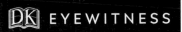

DK EYEWITNESS

W9-AVJ-158

TOP 10
DELHI

Top 10 Delhi Highlights

The Top 10 of Everything

CONTENTS

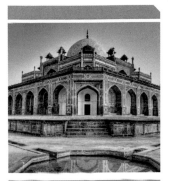

Delhi
Area by Area

Streetsmart

Within each Top 10 list in this book, no hierarchy of quality or popularity is implied. All 10 are, in the editor's opinion, of roughly equal merit.

Title page, front cover and spine
The Diwan-i-Aam audience hall at the Red Fort
Back cover, clockwise from top left
Spices in a local bazaar; India Gate at twilight; Busy Paharganj area; Diwan-i-Aam, Red Fort; Qutb Minar at sunset

Welcome to
Delhi

India's buzzing capital is a metropolis studded with the remains of ancient empires, where exquisite Mughal architecture, grandiose imperial avenues, dazzling modern temples and pretty little mosques jostle for space amid the city's constant bustle, vibrant colours and evocative scents. With Eyewitness Top 10 Delhi, it's yours to explore.

At its heart is **New Delhi**, the British-built imperial city: elegant and spacious, with fine dining and excellent shopping, bisected by the wide, majestic thoroughfare known as the **Rajpath**. The grandiose 17th-century Mughal city of **Old Delhi**, by contrast, is a warren of teeming bazaars concealing all manner of fascinating nooks and crannies, but its magnificent constructions – the famous **Red Fort** complex and the utterly flamboyant **Jama Masjid** mosque among them – are just as impressive as those of the new city.

South of the centre, the **garden tombs of Humayun and Safdarjung** put into context that zenith of Mughal architecture: the **Taj Mahal** in **Agra**, an easy excursion from Delhi, along with the long-abandoned but architecturally rich Mughal city of **Fatehpur Sikri**. Meanwhile, Delhi's modern, efficient and ever-expanding metro system puts into easy reach the scattered sights of **South Delhi** – most notably the 12th-century **Qutb Minar**, which marks the original location of one of the traditional seven cities of Delhi – before heading out to the satellite towns of **Noida** and **Gurgaon (Gurugram)**, burgeoning IT hubs that crackle with the dynamism of an up-and-coming new India.

Whether you're visiting for a weekend or a week, our Top 10 guide brings together the best of everything that Delhi has to offer, from the hottest Indian cuisine to the most magnificent monuments. guide has useful tips throughout, from seeking out what's free avoiding the crowds, plus six easy-to-follow itineraries, desi tie together a clutch of sights in a short space of time. Add photography and detailed maps, and you've got the esse pocket-sized travel companion. **Enjoy the book, and e**

Clockwise from top: Taj Mahal, Baha'i Lotus Temple, Qutb Minar compl Connaught Place, busy Meena Bazaar, the historical India Gate, deta'

Exploring Delhi

There are so many sights to see and things to do in Delhi, you could easily spend a couple of weeks here. Whether you're visiting for a weekend or have the luxury of an extra couple of days, these two- and four-day itineraries will help you make the most of your time in this vibrant city.

The Red Fort offers a glimpse into the opulent lifestyle of the city's former rulers.

Two Days in Delhi

Day ❶
MORNING

From **Khari Baoli** (see p66) market, take a stroll or a cycle-rickshaw down **Chandni Chowk** (see pp14–15) to the **Red Fort** (see pp12–13), before going to see the **Jama Masjid** (see pp16–17).

AFTERNOON

Take an auto-rickshaw to the **Crafts Museum** (see pp28–9), then take a short walk to **Purana Qila** (see p93). From there head to **Humayun's Tomb** (see pp18–19) and **Nizamuddin** (see pp94–5).

Day ❷
MORNING

Start at **Gandhi Smriti** (see p79) and from there walk or take an auto-rickshaw to **Safdarjung's Tomb** (see ... Later, go for a stroll around the ... Lodi Gardens (see pp30–31).

...ON

...to-rickshaw along **Rajpath** ...) from **Rashtrapati** ...dia Gate, before back-... to the **National** ...32–5). Then get the ... Bhawan station ...ng red sandstone ...–7) complex.

Map labels:
St Jar Chur
Qudsia Bagh
Nicholson's Cemetery
Kashmiri Gate
Khari Baoli
Chan Chov
Fatehpuri Masjid
Lal Mandir, Gauri Shankar Man
Jama Masji
Karin
New Delhi station
Connaught Place
TRAIN
Jantar Mantar
Rashtrapati Bhavan
Rajpath
AUTO-RICKSHAW
Udyog Bhawan station
National Museum
Indi Gat
Gandhi Smriti
METRO
AUTO-RICKSHAW
Qutb Minar 9 km (6 miles)
Safdarjung's Tomb
Lodi Garder
METRO
Jorbagh Station
Qutb Minar, Mehrauli Archaeological Park 9 km (6 miles)

Four Days in Delhi

Day ❶
MORNING

See the **Red Fort** (see pp12–13), then pop into the **Lal Mandir** (see p87) and **Gauri Shankar Mandir** (see p88) before walking down **Chandni Chowk** to the **Fatehpuri Masjid** (see p15) and **Khari Baoli** (see p66) market.

AFTERNOON

Take a rickshaw to **Qudsia Bagh** (see p88), then check out **Nicholson's Cemetery** (see p49) and the **Kashmiri Gate** (see p49) before heading past

0 metres 1000
0 yards 1000

British
Residency

Red
Fort

AUTO-RICKSHAW

① Crafts
Museum

Purana
Qila

AUTO-RICKSHAW

Humayun's
Tomb

③
Nizamuddin

Agra,
Fatephur Sikri
210 km (130 miles)

Key

― Two-day itinerary
― Four-day itinerary

The Taj Mahal, Shah Jahan's sublime mausoleum, is a magnificent example of Mughal architecture.

Safdarjung's Tomb features this beautifully decorated arch just above the main entrance.

St James' Church (see p85) and the **British Residency** (see p48) with a cycle-rickshaw to the **Jama Masjid** (see pp16–17), finishing with a mutton *korma* at **Karim's** (see p65).

Day ❷
MORNING
From **Connaught Place** (see p77), head to the **Jantar Mantar** (see p78), then take an auto across **Rajpath** (see pp20–21) to the **National Museum** (see pp32–5).
AFTERNOON
Get an auto-rickshaw to **Rashtrapati Bhavan** (see p21), then another along

Rajpath to **India Gate** (see p20) and **Purana Qila** (see p93). Visit the **Crafts Museum** (see pp28–9).

Day ❸
MORNING
Start at the **Qutb Minar** (see pp24–7), visit the **Mehrauli Archaeological Park** (see pp26–27), then take the metro to **Safdarjung's Tomb** (see p94).
AFTERNOON
Visit **Gandhi Smriti** (see p79) before walking around the **Lodi Gardens** (see pp30–31) and going on to see **Humayun's Tomb** (see pp18–19). Head to **Nizamuddin** (see pp94–5) for the evening's *qawwali* session.

Day ❹
MORNING
Take the morning train to **Agra** and visit the **Taj Mahal** (see pp36–7).
AFTERNOON
Get a taxi to **Fatehpur Sikri** (see p39), before returning to Agra in time to catch the evening train back to Delhi.

Top 10 Delhi Highlights

Visitors at the Taj Mahal
in Agra, Uttar Pradesh

🔟 Delhi Highlights

History is writ large in Delhi, and few places in the world can rival the city's incredible clutch of monuments, spanning 1,000 years of history. These range from the soaring minaret of the Qutb Minar and the imposing Red Fort to the dramatic Jama Masjid and Humayun's Tomb, as well as some of the most grandiose landmarks of the British Raj, such as India Gate.

Red Fort ①
A former residence of the powerful Mughal emperors, the enormous Red Fort is Old Delhi's iconic showpiece attraction, providing a fascinating peek into the cultured world of the country's most charismatic rulers *(see pp12–13)*.

② Chandni Chowk
At the heart of Old Delhi, this famous Mughal thoroughfare, lined with mosques, temples and myriad shops, offers a colourful slice of quintessential Indian street life *(see pp14–15)*.

Jama Masjid ③
The largest and most spectacular mosque in India, this Mughal monument rises out of the streets of Old Delhi *(see pp16–17)*.

④ Humayun's Tomb
The first of the great Mughal garden tombs, this is one of ancient Delhi's most beautiful historical monuments *(see pp18–19)*.

⑤ Rajpath
As the centrepiece of imperial Delhi, this great Raj-era thoroughfare is one of the world's finest examples of Colonial pomp, stretching from the stately India Gate to the grand Rashtrapati Bhavan *(see pp20–21)*.

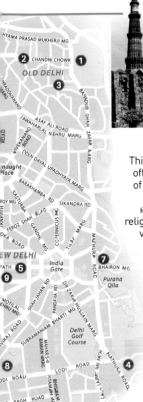

6 **Qutb Minar Complex**

Towering over southern Delhi, the Qutb Minar is perhaps the city's single most dramatic sight, surrounded by monuments from the Sultanate and Mughal periods (see pp24–5).

Crafts Museum **7**

This engaging museum offers a fascinating snapshot of the myriad local arts-and-crafts traditions of the sub-continent, from arcane religious artifacts to traditional village houses (see pp28–9).

8 **Lodi Gardens**

The idyllic Lodi Gardens are dotted with a sequence of atmospheric tombs built in honour of the Delhi sultans. The landscaped grounds make them ideal for a picnic (see pp30–31).

9 **National Museum**

The National Museum is India's finest, with an enormous collection of artifacts and exhibits ranging from the Harappan civilization to the 20th century, covering every aspect of the country's varied cultural history (see pp32–5).

Taj Mahal **10**

Perhaps the most famous – and certainly the most beautiful – monument in the world, the incomparable Taj Mahal in Agra, a masterpiece of Mughal architecture, never fails to astonish and amaze (see pp36–7).

TOP 10 ⭐ Red Fort

In 1638, the Mughal emperor Shah Jahan (r. 1628–58) decided to leave Agra, then capital of the empire, and return to Delhi. Here he created Shahjahanabad, or Old Delhi as it is now known, with the Red Fort (Lal Qila) at its heart. The structure was completed in 1648 and surrounded by enormous red sandstone walls, their colour lending the fort its name. It served as home to the emperor and his successors until the 1857 Uprising. Although time has taken its toll, it remains one of Delhi's most absorbing sights.

1 Naqqar Khana
The second of the fort's major gateways, the Naqqar (or Naubat) Khana was where all visitors were obliged to dismount from their elephants to enter the inner court. In the gallery above, musicians would perform in welcome.

2 Khas Mahal
The emperor's lavishly decorated private apartments are divided by a marble latticework screen surmounted by the scales of justice.

3 Hayat Bakhsh Bagh
North of the Moti Masjid lies the Hayat Bakhsh Bagh, or Life-Bestowing Garden, with two small marble pavilions **(below)** at either end, and the pretty Zafar Mahal, a red sandstone pavilion, in a pool in the middle.

4 Moti Masjid
Built in 1659, the Moti Masjid is closed to visitors, though visitors can peer through its latticed marble screens for a glimpse of the delicate courtyard within.

Red Fort

5 Lahori Gate
The Red Fort's main entrance is the majestic Lahori Gate **(left)**, although its original grandeur has been obscured by the bastion added by Aurangzeb (1618–1707), designed to force attackers into a sideways approach.

6 Diwan-i-Khas
This pillared hall is where the emperor would have conferred with his ministers on affairs of state; it was also where Emperor Shah Jahan's legendary, jewel-encrusted Peacock Throne was housed. It remains easily the most lavish building in the fort, with fine marble carving and pietra dura inlay work.

7 Diwan-i-Aam
One of the Red Fort's most impressive structures, this very elegant sandstone pavilion **(left)** is where the emperor used to hold his public audiences.

THE RED FORT IN THE AGE OF THE MUGHALS

Impressive as it is, what visitors see of the Red Fort today is only a part of the original structure, once a veritable city within a city, with lovely pavilions and gracious courtyards, many of which, sadly, have now vanished. Much of the blame for this falls on the British, who, after the 1857 Uprising, razed many of the fort's grand buildings to the ground. They erected a rather overbearing sequence of barracks in their place which, unfortunately, survive to this day.

9 Shahi Burj and Burj-i-Shamali
The Shahi Burj tower is where water was drawn from the Yamuna River for use within the fort. Aurangzeb later added a fine marble pavilion, called the Burj-i-Shamali, with a water chute leading to a scalloped basin.

NEED TO KNOW

MAP H3 ■ Chandni Chowk ■ Lal Qila Metro; Chandni Chowk Metro ■ asi.nic.in

Open 7am–6pm Tue–Sun (last entry 5pm)

Adm ₹600 (Indians ₹50), video ₹25, audio guides ₹100 plus tax and deposit

■ The sound and light show at the Red Fort is being upgraded. Ask about the status of the show at the entrance.

■ Take a break at the café and visit the museums on the premises.

8 Rang Mahal
The centre of the Red Fort's women's quarters **(above)** has carved marble walls, an inlaid marble fountain and the remains of ornate mirrorwork on the ceiling.

10 Salimgarh Fort
North of the Red Fort is Salimgarh, built in 1546 and later used by the British to imprison independence fighters. It now houses a museum.

🔟⭐ Chandni Chowk

When Shah Jahan built his new city, Chandni Chowk was planned as its principal thoroughfare – a broad, ceremonial avenue leading directly from the Red Fort and a favoured spot for elaborate processions. Most of the street's original buildings are now gone (along with the canal which ran down the middle of the road), but Chandni Chowk, lined with shoebox shops, and eternally bustling with crowds and traffic, retains much of its traditional atmosphere.

1 Gurudwara Sisganj
This large, modern Sikh temple **(above)** commemorates the spot where the ninth Sikh guru, Teg Bahadur, was beheaded on the orders of Mughal emperor Aurangzeb in 1675.

2 Bhai Mati Dass Museum
The museum provides a comprehensive history of the Sikhs in pictures, including some portraits of the ten Sikh gurus.

3 Lal Mandir
Built during the reign of Shah Jahan for the Jain soldiers in his army, the Lal Mandir (Red Temple) is one of Delhi's principal Jain shrines. Made of red Kota stone (hence the name), the temple's towers are major landmarks at the fort end of Chandni Chowk.

4 Town Hall
The elegant British Town Hall **(below)** built in 1864, stands out from cluttered buildings of Chandni Chowk.

NEED TO KNOW

MAP G3 ▪ Chandni Chowk Metro; Lal Qila Metro

▪ The pavements of Chandni Chowk are busy and congested, made worse due to ongoing construction. A rickshaw ride along the road is a fun way to experience this lively area without constantly having to check what's up ahead.

▪ Head to Haldiram's (see p89) for a light meal, or get a tasty parantha from the Paranthe Wali Gali (see p89).

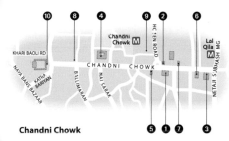

Chandni Chowk

① ⑧ ④ ⑨ ② ⑥
⑤ ① ⑦ ③

CHAINA RAM

Sadly, Chandni Chowk's most famous sweet shop, Ghantewala, established in 1790, closed in 2015. But sweet lovers won't go hungry, because at the street's western end, Chaina Ram, founded in Karachi in 1901, makes the best halwa in India. Its Hindu owner was forced to flee Pakistan in 1947, but in what amounts to a statement against sectarianism, he set up in Delhi's most Muslim neighbourhood.

Narrow streets lined with shops in Chandni Chowk

⑨ Begum Samru's Palace

Half-buried in the middle of a crowded bazaar just off the main street, this huge Neo-Classical mansion (now occupied by the Central Bank of India), was once one of the grandest buildings in Delhi. It was built back in 1823, and had gardens which stretched all the way to Chandni Chowk.

⑤ Sunehri Masjid

This small Mughal mosque (1721) was named for its gilded domes (*sunehri* meaning "golden"). It was from here that Persian invader Nadir Shah watched his soldiers massacre the city's inhabitants in 1739.

⑦ Central Baptist Church

The first Christian mission in northern India when it was founded in 1814 (although the current building dates from 1858), this modest church is an atmospheric memento of the Raj era.

⑩ Fatehpuri Masjid

Located at the far west end of Chandni Chowk, the Fatehpuri Masjid **(below)** was built by a wife of Shah Jahan in 1650, and has an enormous and wonderfully peaceful courtyard.

⑥ Gauri Shankar Mandir

Created for Shankar (Shiva) and Gauri (his wife Parvati), this vibrant Hindu temple features an ancient *lingam*, a symbol of worship of the god Shiva; it is said to be around 800 years old.

⑧ Lala Chunna Mal's Haveli

Built by Hindu merchant Lala Chunna Mal, who had made a fortune supplying British forces in the 1857 Uprising, this sprawling, balconied mansion has no fewer than 128 rooms.

TOP10 ⭐ Jama Masjid

Completed in 1656, the Jama Masjid (Friday Mosque, named after the Muslim day of prayer) is the largest mosque in India, with three huge domes, a pair of minarets over 40 m (131 ft) tall and a courtyard large enough to hold 25,000 worshippers. The mosque is an architectural masterpiece and took six years to build, using 5,000 masons and at a cost of around a million rupees. Today, its soaring minarets and domes are among Old Delhi's most memorable sights.

1 The Façade

The prayer hall's façade **(above)** is the most impressive of any Indian mosque. Ten cusped arches flank the central *iwan* (main arch), indicating the direction of Mecca and providing a focus of prayer to the many worshippers.

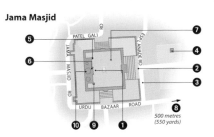

Jama Masjid

2 The Eastern Approach

The most dramatic approach to Jama Masjid is from the east, between the busy stalls of the Meena Bazaar, with the grand mosque looming ahead.

3 Meena Bazaar

This busy market on the eastern approach sells prayer rugs, framed Koranic inscriptions and numerous other Islamic items **(left)**, amid the smoky scent of freshly cooked kebabs from the dozens of nearby *dhabas*.

4 Tomb of Maulana Azad

Halfway along Meena Bazaar, an opening on the right leads up to a raised tomb that houses the remains of Maulana Azad (1888–1958), a major figure in the fight for Indian independence.

6 Prayer Hall
On the western side of the courtyard is the enormous *liwan*, or prayer hall. Its western wall is punctuated by no fewer than seven *mihrabs*, niches that indicate the direction of Mecca to worshippers. A graceful *minbar*, or pulpit, stands to the right.

7 The Courtyard
Designed as a place to go for communal worship, the enormous, breezy courtyard **(below)** has space for thousands of religious worshippers.

SHAH JAHAN: MASTER BUILDER

Mughal emperor Shah Jahan was a prolific builder, who during his 30-year reign, promoted an architectural outpouring that has never been matched. In addition to Delhi's Jama Masjid and the Red Fort, he commissioned extensive additions to the Agra Fort *(see p38)*, and oversaw a spate of construction in Lahore, Pakistan (including the Shalimar Gardens), not to mention the superb Taj Mahal *(see pp36–7)*

9 South Minaret Views
The South Minaret affords unrivalled views **(below)** of Old Delhi. There are about 120 narrow steps and not much space at the top.

6 The Minarets
The main prayer hall is framed by two brick minarets. Their slender outlines add a much needed lightness to the long, arcaded façade, which is topped with bulbous Hindu-style *chattris* (pavilions).

8 Pataudi House Mosque
This is one of Delhi's prettiest little mosques – white with triple domes and frilly doorways. It dates as far back as the 18th century, when it was part of a *haveli*, that is now long gone.

NEED TO KNOW

MAP H4 ■ Off Netaji Subhash Marg ■ 011 2336 5358 ■ Chawri Bazaar Metro; Jama Masjid Metro

Open 8am daily until 30 minutes before sunset (at certain times of the day visitors may need to wait for prayers to finish)

Camera ₹300

■ Female visitors should be accompanied by a man, but this rule is not followed strictly.

■ Dress respectfully – no shorts, short skirts or sleeveless tops. It is a good idea to come with appropriate clothing, although overgarments are provided if needed.

■ You cannot eat or drink within the mosque itself, but Karim's *(see p89)* is close by, and there are many roadside cafés.

10 The Domes
Three huge onion domes sit atop the main prayer hall, their bulbous outlines picked out in delicate black stripes. The central dome is partially obscured by the massive *iwan* in front, an architectural conundrum that even Shah Jahan's master architects were unable to resolve.

TOP 10 ⭐ Humayun's Tomb

Built in the 1560s, this gigantic mausoleum is the first of the great Mughal garden tombs and the final resting place of the ill-fated emperor Humayun (r. 1530–40 and 1555–6). The mausoleum is one of Delhi's most impressive sights and a classic example of the tradition of tomb-building which, almost 100 years later, was to reach its zenith in the Taj Mahal. It is also one of the most peaceful places in Delhi, with a huge expanse of beautiful gardens and an absorbing cluster of further tombs, gateways and mosques.

1 The Western Gateway

The entrance to the gardens is through the western gateway **(left)**. This serves as a kind of architectural curtain, designed to conceal the garden and tomb from the visitor's view until the very last minute, when Humayun's magnificent mausoleum appears in all its glory.

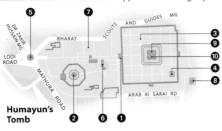

Humayun's Tomb

2 Mosque and Tomb of Isa Khan

The florid octagonal mosque and tomb of Isa Khan **(below)**, a courtier during the reign of Sher Shah Suri (r. 1540–45), provides a complete change of style. Both mosque and tomb lie within their own garden, enclosed in fortress-like walls.

3 The Gardens

The beautiful gardens that surround the tomb follow the Persian-style *charbagh* pattern, in which the garden is divided into four quarters by water channels: a representation of the Islamic gardens of paradise.

4 The Barber's Tomb

According to legend, this elegant tomb was built for the imperial barber – a rather fitting memorial to the person who was trusted to hold a razor to the emperor's throat.

5 Sabz Burj

Housing the grave of an unknown Mughal nobleman, this beautiful blue-domed, Persian-style tomb now stands marooned on a busy roundabout near the entrance to the complex.

8 Nila Gumbad

The striking Persian-style Nila Gumbad, with its blue-tiled dome, houses the remains of an unknown Mughal nobleman.

9 The Tomb

Set atop a large raised platform, the mausoleum is topped by a massive dome. Each of its four façades is dominated by a huge arch.

HUMAYUN

The second Mughal emperor, Humayun, was an endearingly irresolute figure, who alternated between bouts of utter military brilliance and total self-indulgence. After succeeding his father Babur in 1530, he lost his empire to the Afghan invader Sher Shah Suri, and was obliged to seek refuge in Persia for the next 15 years – until he won the empire back. His luck didn't last: one year later he was dead, having fallen down a very steep flight of steps in the Purana Qila (see p93).

6 The Arab Serai

This extensive walled garden is where visiting craftsmen are thought to have lived while they worked on the tomb. It also houses the neat little Afsarwala Mosque and Tomb (above).

7 Bu Halima's Garden

The entrance to the complex is through Bu Halima's garden, which has its own gateway. This gateway pre-dates the tomb itself, although the mausoleum and the garden were designed in alignment to it.

10 The Interior

A single door on the southern side opens into the mausoleum's interior (right), where Humayun lies in a small, plain marble tomb.

NEED TO KNOW

MAP S6 ■ Off Mathura Road ■ Taxi, auto-rickshaw or Nizamuddin Metro

Open Sunrise–sunset daily

Adm ₹600, card/online ₹550 (Indians ₹40, ₹35 card/online), video ₹50

···

■ Walking clockwise around the exterior of the tomb before going inside gives a sense of the scale of the mausoleum. The walk also takes in the Barber's Tomb and Nila Gumbad, after which the tomb can be entered via the southern entrance.

■ There is also a small museum set inside the Western Gateway.

🔟⭐ Around Rajpath

Running east to west through the heart of New Delhi, Rajpath (formerly Kingsway) is the grandest of all the city's boulevards, stretching 2 km (1 mile) from India Gate to the presidential palace, Rashtrapati Bhavan. Rajpath was created to showcase spectacular processions and occasions of state, while the surrounding central government buildings were intended to serve as an enduring symbol of British pomp and power to rival – or, indeed, surpass – those monuments left scattered around the city by previous rulers.

3 Cathedral Church of the Redemption

Designed by Henry Medd, assistant to British architect Herbert Baker (1862–1946), this 1935 Neo-Classical church **(left)** was largely inspired by Andrea Palladio's Il Redentore in Venice, and is one of the biggest, most impressive churches in Delhi.

1 Secretariat Buildings

Flanking Raisina Hill are the Secretariat Buildings. Designed by Herbert Baker in Neo-Classical style with Indian touches, they now house local government offices.

4 Raisina Hill

The area of Raisina Hill rises between the Secretariat Buildings towards Rashtrapati Bhavan, although the latter only becomes visible once you reach the top, a miscalculation that infuriated Lutyens.

2 India Gate

This imposing arch commemorates the 90,000 Indian soldiers killed in World War I and the Afghan Wars. Below the arch, the Tomb of the Unknown Soldier **(below)** honours those who died during the 1971 Indo-Pakistan conflict.

5 Rajpath

This grand 2-km (1-mile) axis **(above)** connects India Gate with Rashtrapati Bhavan, linking many of New Delhi's major buildings along the way.

6 Sansad Bhavan

Built for the Legislative Assembly in 1935, this distinctive circular building to the north of Rajpath is now home to the Indian parliament. It is set at a distance from Rajpath, reflecting Britain's grudging attitude towards India's democratic aspirations.

Around Rajpath

7 Mughal Gardens
Set within the grounds of Rashtrapati Bhavan, this beautiful oasis is laid out with watercourses, fountains and neat squares of manicured lawn.

8 Rashtrapati Bhavan
Once the viceroy's residence and now home to the President of India, the magnificent Rashtrapati Bhavan is Edwin Lutyens' masterpiece, a uniquely successful fusion of European and Indian elements. Visitors can register in advance for a guided tour.

9 Military Parades
The Republic Day parade on 26 January features a dazzling show of military personnel (left) and brightly coloured floats from some Indian states. Festivities eventually come to a close with Beating the Retreat, a wonderful, ceremonious performance of military bands held on Raisina Hill on 29 January.

10 Vijay Chowk
Formerly known as the Grand Place, Vijay Chowk is an enormous crossroads marking the point at which Rajpath meets Raisina Hill.

NEED TO KNOW
MAP L3 ■ Central Secretariat Metro & Udyog Bhawan Metro

Rashtrapati Bhavan: 2301 5321 (tours); www.rashtrapatisachivalaya.gov.in/rbtour

■ The main government buildings on Rajpath, which include Sansad Bhavan as well as the Secretariat, are closed to the public. The roads around Sansad Bhavan are also closed; the Cathedral Church of the Redemption is accessible from the north.

■ There are places to eat and drink along Rajpath. Some of the grassy areas that flank Rajpath are good picnic spots. The National Museum (see p32) has a pleasant café.

Following pages Jama Masjid in Old Delhi

⭐ Qutb Minar Complex

Towering over southern Delhi, the monumental Qutb Minar is one of the city's most dramatic and instantly recognizable landmarks: a triumphal minaret that marked, with a flourish, both the coming of Islam to the subcontinent and the arrival of the Delhi sultans, who held power in northern India for around 400 years. Further remarkable monuments, including India's oldest mosque, lie scattered at the foot of the minaret and nearby, around Mehrauli village.

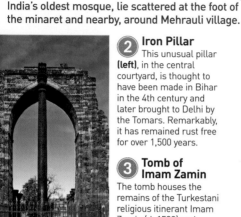

② Iron Pillar

This unusual pillar **(left)**, in the central courtyard, is thought to have been made in Bihar in the 4th century and later brought to Delhi by the Tomars. Remarkably, it has remained rust free for over 1,500 years.

③ Tomb of Imam Zamin

The tomb houses the remains of the Turkestani religious itinerant Imam Zamin (d. 1539) and postdates the Qutb Minar complex.

① Quwwat-ul-Islam

The first mosque in Delhi, the Quwwat-ul-Islam (Might of Islam), was built by Qutbuddin Aibak (r. 1206–10) in 1192, soon after Muhammad Ghori's conquest *(see p42)* of northwest India.

④ Qutb Minar

Built during the reigns of Aibak and Iltutmish (r. 1211–36), this tapering minaret **(right)** is 72 m (236 ft) tall. A fifth storey, clad in marble, was added later, after the summit was damaged by lightning.

8 Madrasa of Alauddin Khilji

Built around 1317 as a *madrasa* (religious school), this plain building **(left)** has lost most of its original stone facing. Alauddin (r. 1296–1316) himself is thought to be buried in its central chamber.

9 Alai Minar

A large stump of rough stone is all that remains of a rather maverick scheme to build a second oversized minaret, intended to be even greater than the mighty Qutb Minar.

5 Tomb of Iltutmish

Immediately behind the mosque is the tomb of Iltutmish, one of the principal architects of the Qutb Minar complex. Small and plain on the outside, the tomb is lavishly carved within.

6 Alai Darwaza

Built in 1311 as a brand new gateway to the mosque, the Alai Darwaza is richly carved using red sandstone and white marble, a hallmark of the later Mughal style.

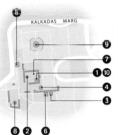

Qutb Minar Complex

10 The Prayer Hall Screen

One of the finest pieces of Islamic architecture in all of India, the Quwwat ul-Islam's prayer hall screen **(left)** is composed of five sharply pointed arches that are covered in Koranic inscriptions and floral decoration.

7 The Central Courtyard

Aibak demolished 27 Hindu and Jain temples to make way for his mosque. The temple pillars were incorporated into the arcade of the central courtyard **(below)**, giving it a Hindu appearance.

THE TOWER OF BABEL, DELHI STYLE

The Alai Minar was the brainchild of Alauddin Khilji, the most brilliant and ruthless of all the Delhi sultans. The plan was to build a minaret twice the height of the Qutb Minar, but the gargantuan project never really got off the ground, and all that remains is a large pile of rubble – "a frustrated tower of Babel", as one writer describes it.

NEED TO KNOW

MAP U3 ■ Mehrauli, Delhi-Gurugram Road ■ Taxi, auto-rickshaw or Qutab Minar Metro

Open Sunrise–sunset daily

Adm ₹600, card/online ₹550 (Indians ₹40, card/online ₹35), video ₹50, audio guide ₹100 plus tax and a deposit of ID, credit card or ₹2,000

....

■ Arrive early or late to avoid the coach parties.

■ There are drink stalls around the entrance to the complex. For food, it is best to bring a picnic.

Sites around Mehrauli

The beautiful and intricately designed Rajon ki Bain stepwell

1 Rajon ki Bain
Built in 1506, this superb *baoli* (stepwell) is atmospherically buried amid woodland in the heart of the park. It has been built up over four levels, with rooms and arcades around the top two floors and a well situated at the bottom.

2 Jamali-Kamali Masjid and Tomb
This beautiful early Mughal mosque, built by the poet Sheikh Fazlullah (known as Jamali; d. 1535), has a delicately carved façade and characteristic red sandstone and white marble stonework. The poet's tomb is located in an enclosure beside the mosque.

Ceiling detail, Jamali-Kamali Tomb

3 Adham Khan's Tomb
Mughal emperor Akbar built this tomb for his foster brother, who was thrown to his death from Agra Fort's battlements for murdering Akbar's prime minister. The tomb's labyrinthine interior has earned it the nickname *bhulbhulaiyan* (maze).

4 Quli Khan's Tomb
Erected for Adham Khan's brother, Mohammad Quli Khan, this neat little tomb was converted into a summer retreat by Sir Thomas Metcalfe. It was christened Dilkusha, or "Heart's Delight"; the ruined walls can still be seen around the tomb.

5 Balban's Tomb
Close to the Jamali-Kamali Masjid lie the fragments of the tomb of Balban (1200–87), one of the most powerful of the early Delhi sultans.

6 Madhi Masjid
Constructed in the early Mughal era, this heavily fortified building looks more like a fortress than a mosque, with a large courtyard and – unusually – two separate prayer halls on either side of a central *mihrab* wall.

7 Dargah Qutb Sahib
In the heart of the Mehrauli bazaar (ask locally for directions), this serene little religious complex

honours Qutbuddin Bakhtiyar Kaki (d. 1235), a Sufi saint from Fergana (in modern Uzbekistan), and contains his grave, among other buildings.

8 Zafar Mahal

This summer palace was built by Emperor Akbar Shah II (1760–1837) and contains various structures, including Moti Masjid and the tombs of two Mughal emperors.

A courtyard within the Jahaz Mahal

Sites around Mehrauli

9 Jahaz Mahal

At the western end of Mehrauli village, this enigmatic Lodi-era structure is thought to have been either a travellers' rest house or an opulent royal pleasure palace.

10 Mehrauli Archaeological Park

West of the Qutb, this park was set up to protect the ancient monuments dotted around the area, including over 70, dating from the 11th to the 19th centuries, in the park itself.

METCALFE'S FOLLY

Mehrauli witnessed one of the stranger episodes in Anglo-Indian history when Sir Thomas Theophilus Metcalfe (1795–1853), British Resident at the Mughal Court, decided to establish a summer residence in the area. Rather than build a new house, Metcalfe made the unusual decision to convert the tomb of Quli Khan into an English-style country residence, which he christened Dilkusha (Heart's Delight), although it is generally known as Metcalfe's Folly. The tomb's central chamber was turned into a dining room, a pair of flanking wings and various outbuildings were erected (remnants of which can still be seen), and a string of Indian-style follies were built in the surrounding countryside, including a prominent *chattri* (open-sided pavilion) on a nearby hill. As fate would have it, Metcalfe's love of all things Mughal did him little good: he died slowly, allegedly poisoned by one of the emperor's queens.

The Mughal tomb of Quli Khan

TOP 10 ⬤ Crafts Museum

This enjoyable museum showcases India's incredible variety of local artistic and cultural traditions in a rustic building and walled garden designed by Charles Correa (1930–2015). There are some wonderful, fascinating crafts here from every part of the subcontinent and in every medium, from tribal costumes to ivory carvings. There is even a complete miniature village of traditional buildings from across India in the grounds outside.

③ Folk and Tribal Art

This gallery **(left)** is packed with unusual objects dating from the 19th century to the present day, from a collection of traditional dolls to religious items.

④ Outdoor Exhibits

A number of exhibits are dotted around the Crafts Museum grounds, such as stone carvings from Rajasthan and a striking group of Indo-Chinese statues from Tamil Nadu.

NEED TO KNOW

MAP R3 ▪ Bhairon Marg ▪ 233 71370 ▪ Pragati Maidan Metro

Open 10am–5pm Tue–Sun

Adm ₹200 (Indians ₹20), camera ₹500

▪ The museum is good for crafts shopping, but do research beforehand. It is best to visit the government emporiums around Connaught Place to see what is available and get an idea of prices.

▪ Permission to take photographs can be obtained from reception.

▪ Visit Café Lota (78389 60787), inside the museum, known for its fusion Indian cuisine and teas and coffees.

① Museum Building

Designed by Indian architect Charles Correa, this rustic, ochre-coloured building, encircled by shady verandahs and set in a tree-filled compound, feels like a rural village in the heart of Delhi.

② Resident Craftspeople

The small courtyard, at the back of the museum, is home to a selection of stalls. Artisans can often be seen at work on a wide range of crafts, such as painting, stone carving, metalworking and weaving. They also sell their products.

⑤ Cultic Objects Gallery

This gallery houses religious objects from across India, ranging from Hindu bronzes and South Indian paintings to unique Jain and Tibetan Buddhist artifacts.

⑥ Bhuta Sculpture Gallery

Devoted to the Bhuta cult of Karnataka, this gallery **(left)** contains images from the shrine of Nandikeshvara in Udipi province, carved in dark jackfruit wood and featuring striking human and animal-headed figures.

8 Traditional Buildings

Scattered around the museum garden is a fascinating collection of traditional buildings from across India, including a traditional house **(left)** from Kullu in the state of Himachal Pradesh.

GALLERY GUIDE

The Crafts Museum is relatively small and can be covered in a couple of hours. All the galleries are laid out over the ground floor of the building, except the Textile Gallery and a section of the Courtly Crafts Gallery, which are tucked away upstairs and can be easy to miss.

---

7 Textile Gallery

10 Courtly Crafts Gallery

Key to Floorplan

- Ground floor
- First floor

10 Courtly Crafts Gallery

5 Cultic Objects Gallery

2 Resident Craftspeople

8 Traditional Buildings

1 The Museum Building

6 Bhuta Sculpture Gallery

3 Folk and Tribal Art

9 Shopping for Crafts

Crafts Museum

7 Textile Gallery

This beautiful, well-curated gallery provides an overview of India's textile traditions, with a vast collection of fabrics in styles including brocade, block printing, tie-dye and appliqué.

9 Shopping for Crafts

The museum has one of Delhi's most interesting selections of traditional crafts for sale, either from one of the stalls at the back of the museum **(below)**, or the shop.

10 Courtly Crafts Gallery

Aristocratic arts from the 18th century to today are displayed here, including *bidri*-ware (silver inlay work) **(above)**, enamel-ware, jade, ivory carvings and glass jewellery.

⊞10 ⭐ Lodi Gardens

One of the most enjoyable excursions in Delhi, the beautiful Lodi Gardens offer a winning combination of nature and history. The gardens themselves are among the most attractive and relaxed in the city, with quiet paths winding between tropical trees and plentiful birdlife in the branches overhead. The series of fine medieval tombs dotted among the trees and lawns, erected by nobles of the Lodi and Sayyid Dynasties during the later years of the Delhi Sultanate, provide historical interest.

② Muhammad Shah's Tomb

The tomb (**left**) of Sayyid ruler Muhammad Shah (r. 1434–44) is built in the octagonal shape favoured by the later Delhi sultans. Its main dome is surrounded by eight small *chattris*.

③ The Gardens

The gardens were created in 1936 by Lady Willingdon, wife of the viceroy and governor-general of India. She had the two villages that stood here demolished to make way for the new gardens.

① Sikander Lodi's Tomb

At the northern end of the gardens is the tomb of Sikander Lodi (r. 1489–1517), the penultimate Delhi sultan. It occupies an idyllic garden and has interior walls that feature the remains of the original blue tilework.

THE SAYYID AND LODI DYNASTIES

The Sayyid and Lodi Dynasties held sway from 1414 until 1526, though their power was challenged by a series of internal rebellions and external threats. The first Sayyid sultan, Khizr Khan, rose to power after Timur's invasion in 1398; while the last sultan, Ibrahim Lodi (r. 1517–26), was killed by Timur's great-great-great-grandson, Babur, who was the founder of the Mughal Dynasty.

④ National Bonsai Garden

Near the southern entrance to the park, the National Bonsai Garden sports a collection of tiny trees. A few displays show the various styles of traditional bonsai.

⑤ Athpula

Located near the tomb of Sikander Lodi, the striking, graceful Athpula (Eight Piers) bridge (**above**) was built during the reign of Mughal emperor Akbar (r. 1556–1605).

6 Shish Gumbad
Built around 1600 for an unidentified nobleman, this is a cuboid-shaped tomb **(below)**, enlivened with bands of rich blue tiles, which run around the middle and top.

8 Bara Gumbad Masjid
Attached to the Bara Gumbad Tomb, this mosque is small but lavishly decorated, with swirls of Koranic script **(right)** covering every available surface.

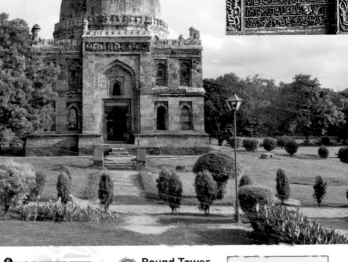

Lodi Gardens

9 Round Tower
To the east of the Bara Gumbad stands a solid-looking round tower, probably built during the 14th century.

10 Bara Gumbad Tomb
Dating from around 1500, the Bara Gumbad Tomb is the gardens' most impressive structure, a cuboid tomb (occupant unknown), topped by a massive dome. Its rather severe outlines are relieved by alternating panels of red and black stone.

7 Birdlife
The gardens are home to a rich array of birdlife, including tree pies, blue throats, spotted owlets, geese and green parakeets **(right)**.

NEED TO KNOW

MAP N6 ■ Lodi Road ■ Taxi, auto-rickshaw or Jor Bagh Metro

Open Apr–Sep: 5am–8pm daily; Oct–Mar: 6am–8pm daily

National Bonsai Garden: open 9am–5pm Mon–Sat; closed public hols

■ There is nowhere to eat or drink within the gardens, but you are welcome to bring a picnic with you.

■ The India Habitat Centre, near the southern entrance on Lodi Road, has a couple of attractive cafés.

🔟⭐ National Museum

Founded in 1949, the superb National Museum is India's finest, with a collection of over 200,000 exhibits charting five millennia of subcontinental history. Every major strand in India's complex cultural identity is covered here, with artifacts from across the country and beyond, including prehistoric archaeological finds, Buddhist statues, Chola bronzes and Mughal miniatures.

① Mughal Emperor Shah Jahan in Dara Shikoh's Marriage Procession

Painted around 1750 in Awadh, this painting **(below)** is a good example of superbly detailed Indian miniature art, portraying the wedding procession of Shah Jahan's favourite son, Dara Shikoh.

④ Dancing Girl

This small but famous image of an elegant, long-legged dancing girl **(left)** was found in Mohenjodaro. Dating from around 2500 BC, it is one of the world's oldest cast-bronze statuettes.

② Harappan Bronze Chariot

One of the museum's most charming pieces is a bronze figurine (c. 2000 BC) of a man on a chariot pulled by oxen.

③ Avalokitesvara

These rare 9th- and 10th-century silk paintings, from the town of Dunhuang on the old Silk Route in northwestern China, depict Avalokitesvara, the Bodhisattva of Infinite Compassion, a deity of Vajrayana Buddhism.

⑤ Ganga

This 5th-century Gupta terracotta statue **(below)** is one of the museum's most graceful. The river goddess Ganga is seen walking on the back of her mythical animal mount, the crocodile-like *makara*, whilst carrying an urn.

NEED TO KNOW

MAP N3 ■ 11 Janpath, just south of Rajpath ■ 2301 9272 ■ Udyog Bhawan Metro ■ www.nationalmuseumindia.gov.in

Open 11am–6:30pm Tue–Fri, 11am–8pm Sat & Sun; closed public hols

Adm ₹650 (Indians ₹20), audio guide free with a deposit of ID (Indians ₹150 for an English audio guide)

■ The museum regularly closes areas or galleries for renovation. It is best to call ahead or check the website first.

■ The collection is huge, so don't try to see everything at once. An audio guide picks around 30 of the best exhibits.

■ The film show runs Tue–Sun at 11:30am, 2:30pm and 4pm.

■ There is a small café on the museum premises.

GALLERY GUIDE

The museum collection is arranged over three floors, although almost all of the best exhibits are to be found on the ground floor of the building. The first nine exhibits described here are displayed on the ground floor, while the tenth is on the first floor. The museum's film show on Art and Culture is a must-see. Near the museum's reception area, there is also a shop, with books and replicas of some of the exhibits for sale. A visit to the extensive library can be valuable for researchers.

⑦ Shiva Nataraja

This iconic 12th-century Chola bronze **(left)** shows Shiva as *nataraj* ("lord of dance"), surrounded by a ring of fire, representing the cycle of life. He is performing *tandava*, the cosmic dance of destruction and creation

⑥ Mughal Nativity Painting

This Muslim version of a usually Christian subject **(below)** may seem surprising, but Jesus is revered as a prophet by Muslims, and Mary is mentioned more in the Koran than in the Bible.

⑧ Baluchari Sari

Rare 18th-century silk saris with delicate floral patterns are part of the collection. They were made in Murshidabad (West Bengal), one of the country's most famous silk production centres.

⑩ Kali

The fearsome goddess Kali, one of the more favoured deities of the Cholas, appears serenely poised and unusually benign in an outstanding late 12th-century bronze.

Asita's Visit to Suddhadhana ⑨

This is a beautifully carved stone bas-relief **(right)** from the great Satavahana-era Buddhist monastery of Amaravati (Andhra Pradesh), dating from the 1st–2nd century AD. The panel depicts the sage Asita visiting King Suddhadhana in the town of Lumbini to admire his son, the newly born Buddha.

National Museum Collections

Key to Floorplan
- Ground floor
- First floor
- Second floor

National Museum Collections

1 Kushan (Gandhara, Mathura and Ikshavaku Art)

This superb collection of classical sculpture from the Gandhara kingdom (in Afghanistan) is famous for its remarkable Indo-Greek culture, in which local Buddhist traditions intermingled with the Greek styles brought to the region by Alexander the Great (356–23 BC).

2 Gupta Terracotta and Early Medieval Art

The classic art of the Guptas (3rd–5th centuries), the second of India's great dynasties, is on show here, alongside some of the more flamboyant statues from the early Pallava (300–900 AD) and Chola (300 BC–1279 AD) kingdoms of the south, featuring beautiful, intricately carved Hindu gods.

3 Bronzes

This is one of the museum's highlights: a room full of Chola bronze statues of Hindu deities, including one of the most iconic images of Indian art – a pair of Shiva *natarajas*.

4 Late Medieval Art

Outstanding examples of the sculptural arts that flourished across central and southern India during the 11th and 12th centuries feature in this excellent collection, including those from the Vijayanagar, Hoysala, Chola and Pala kingdoms.

5 Harappan Civilization

The museum is one of the world's finest showcases of artifacts from the Harappan (or Indus Valley) Civilization (circa 2500–1500 BC). On display are a wide range of finds from Harappa, Mohenjodaro and elsewhere, vividly bringing one of the world's most ancient cultures to life.

6 Indian Miniature Paintings

Another of the museum's highlights, this is an extensive collection of superbly detailed and vibrant paintings from the schools of Rajasthani, Pahari, Deccani and Mughal.

7 Maurya, Sunga and Satavahana Art

These galleries are devoted to the art of the Mauryans (321–185 BC), India's first great empire, and their successors. Displays include monumental sculptures, bas-relief carvings and stone pillars, most recovered

Sunga sculpture of an amorous couple

INDIAN MINIATURE PAINTING

Although originally of Persian origin, the art of the miniature was perfected in India, where artists developed a distinctive style of brilliantly coloured and minutely detailed painting, usually depicting either religious subjects or scenes from courtly life. Miniature painting flourished under Muslim patronage throughout India – the Mughals, in particular, commissioned thousands of pictures and illustrated manuscripts, while distinctive regional schools subsequently developed in Rajasthan, the Deccan and across the Pahari region in the Himalayan foothills. Most artists remain anonymous, although a few of the most famous are listed on the right

TOP 10
MINIATURE PAINTERS

1 Mir Sayyid Ali (Persian/Mughal, 16th century)

2 Abd al-Samad (Persian/Mughal, 16th century)

3 Basawan (Mughal, 16th century)

4 Mansur (Mughal, 17th century)

5 Bishandas (Mughal, 17th century)

6 Abu al-Hasan (Mughal, 17th century)

7 Govardhan (Mughal, 17th century)

8 Bichitr (Mughal, 17th century)

9 Sahibdin (Rajasthan, 17th century)

10 Dalchand (Rajasthan, 18th century)

Miniature painting (1725–30) from Bundi, Rajasthan, depicting ladies playing *chaupar*, National Museum

from Buddhist temples, including panels from the Buddhist monastery of Amaravati in Andhra Pradesh *(see p33)*.

8 Decorative Arts and Textiles

Dedicated to India's rich and varied clothing and textile traditions, this gallery features a colourful display of woven, printed, tie-dyed, embroidered and appliqué-worked fabrics in silk, cotton and wool. Examples of India's varied decorative arts, including exquisite artifacts made from ivory, jade, glass, ceramic and wood, fill the adjoining galleries.

Silver-incised bowl, Decorative Arts Gallery

9 Tribal Lifestyle

This is a rare glimpse into the lives of India's little-known, Chinese-descended north-eastern tribes. Exhibits include simple weapons, household items and some unusual headgear, backed up by fascinating black-and-white photos of tribes in traditional attire.

10 Buddhist Art

A wide range of Buddhist art and arti-facts from across India, Nepal, Gandhara and China are on display here, including some rare *thangkas* (devotional paintings), statues and a pair of fine silver-and-brass temple trumpets from Ladakh.

TOP 10 ⭐ Taj Mahal, Agra and Fatehpur Sikri

In 1504, Sikandar Lodi moved his capital from Delhi to Agra. Shah Jahan moved it back in 1638, but when his favourite wife – Mumtaz (or "Taj") Mahal – died before the move, the grief-stricken emperor had this magnificent tomb built for her in Agra. Of unparalleled beauty, the Taj is the zenith of Mughal architecture. Agra has other wonderful Mughal structures, and just down the road, Shah Jahan's grandfather, Akbar, had an entire city built at Fatehpur Sikri.

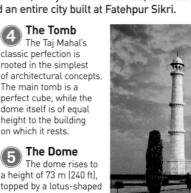

4 The Tomb
The Taj Mahal's classic perfection is rooted in the simplest of architectural concepts. The main tomb is a perfect cube, while the dome itself is of equal height to the building on which it rests.

1 The Charbagh
The Taj sits at the far end of one of the finest Mughal *charbagh*-style gardens (above), an expanse of lawn divided into four by raised marble water channels.

2 Chowk-i-Jilo Khana
The Chowk-i-Jilo Khana is a forecourt. At its northern edge is a gateway, which leads to the Taj but screens it from the view of those outside.

5 The Dome
The dome rises to a height of 73 m (240 ft), topped by a lotus-shaped design and surrounded by four smaller *chattris* (domed pavilions), echoing those that cap the four minarets.

6 Minarets
Minarets mark each of the four corners. Unusually, these are detached from the main tomb, so that if any of them ever fell, they would collapse away from the principal structure.

7 The Lotus Pool
The centre of the *charbagh's* four intersecting water channels is marked by the marble Lotus Pool, symbolizing the pool in the Islamic gardens of paradise.

8 Calligraphic Panels
Koranic inscriptions frame the tomb's four archways. The script in the higher panels has been enlarged to compensate for the distorting effects of perspective.

3 Tomb Chamber
The tomb of Mumtaz Mahal (below) sits at the centre of the atmospheric tomb chamber, and is protected by an exquisitely detailed *jali* (carved screen), while the tomb of Shah Jahan lies alongside it.

9 Mosque and Mehman Khana
The Taj is flanked by two mirror-image buildings: a mosque **(above)** and the Mehman Khana, or *jawab* (response). The *jawab* cannot be used for worship since it is oriented the wrong way round.

THE BLACK TAJ

Of the many strange myths surrounding the Taj, the most frequently repeated is that Shah Jahan intended to build a black marble Taj for himself, set across the Yamuna River from the original. The idea was first mooted by visiting Frenchman Jean-Baptiste Tavernier (1605–89) in 1665. There is, however, no evidence to support this appealing but fanciful theory.

Taj Mahal, a masterpiece of unparalleled beauty

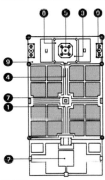

Taj Mahal

NEED TO KNOW

MAP C3

Taj Mahal: Taj Ganj, Agra, 215 km (134 miles) SE of Delhi; open 30 min before sunrise–30 min before sunset Sat–Thu; adm varies, check website for details; www.tajmahal.gov.in

Fatehpur Sikri: 45 km (28 miles) SW of Agra; open sunrise–sunset daily; adm ₹610 (Indians ₹50), video ₹25 (the Jama Masjid and the museum are free to enter)

■ Arrive early at the Taj to avoid the crowds. Security is tight and visitors cannot bring in food, drink (apart from a bottle of water), phones or even guidebooks. There are a number of cafés outside in Taj Ganj.

■ Fatehpur Sikri's small Archaeological Museum (open 9am–5pm Sat–Thu) has artifacts from before Fatehpur Sikri was built.

10 Pietra Dura
Large parts of the Taj Mahal's exterior walls are covered in excellent pietra dura inlay **(above)**, in which intricate stylized geometrical floral patterns are created using coloured precious and semiprecious stones.

Sights in Agra

1 Sikandra
MAP C3 ■ Open sunrise–sunset daily ■ Adm

The huge mausoleum of Sikandra is one of the grandest of all the Mughal monuments, although something of an architectural hotch-potch, with the usual rooftop dome replaced with a strange four-storey pavilion.

The tomb of Akbar, Sikandra

2 Taj Nature Walk
MAP C3 ■ Open summer: 7am–7pm daily; winter: 8am–5pm daily ■ Adm ■ www.tajmahal.gov.in

This is an attractive area of wooded parkland, with views of the Taj itself.

3 Mehtab Bagh
MAP C3 ■ Open sunrise–sunset daily ■ Adm

The Moonlight Garden offers the ultimate view of the Taj Mahal.

4 Itimad-ud-Daulah
MAP C3 ■ Open sunrise–sunset daily ■ Adm

Built by Nur Jahan (1577–1645), this tomb is decorated with pietra dura.

5 Agra Fort
MAP C3 ■ Open sunrise–sunset daily ■ Adm and charge for video

The Agra Fort was originally built by Akbar (1542–1605) and enlarged and embellished by Jahangir (1569–1627) and Shah Jahan.

6 Jama Masjid
MAP C3 ■ Open sunrise–sunset daily

Built in 1648, this spectacular mosque, topped with a trio of domes, is a perfect example of the late-Mughal architectural style perfected during the reign of Shah Jahan.

7 Kinari Bazaar
MAP C3 ■ Open 11:30am–6pm Mon–Sat

This atmospheric bazaar is home to the city's purveyors of *petha*, an unusual confection made from crystallized pumpkin.

8 Chini-ka-Rauza
MAP C3 ■ Open daily

This Persian-style tomb (1628-39) was built for Afzal Khan, a poet who served as Shah Jahan's minister.

9 Rambagh Gardens
MAP C3 ■ Open sunrise–sunset daily ■ Adm

These formal gardens are laid out in the traditional Persian *charbagh* plan.

10 Mariam's Tomb
MAP C3 ■ Open sunrise–sunset daily ■ Adm

This pretty tomb was built in honour of Mariam Zamani, one of Akbar's wives and mother of Jahangir.

Itimad-ud-Daulah

Sights in Fatehpur Sikri

Visitors outside the impressive Jama Masjid on a sunny day

1 Jama Masjid
The magnificent Jama Masjid, one of the biggest mosques in India, houses the tomb of the Sufi saint Salim Chisti. It is entered through a massive, spectacular gate called the Buland Darwaza, which leads into the mosque's huge courtyard.

2 Diwan-i-Aam
The emperor received ordinary subjects in this courtyard, whose colonnade is topped with Hindu-style capitals. The emperor sat in a small pavilion flanked by carved screens.

3 Diwan-i-Khas
The emperor's private audience hall deliberately combines Muslim, Hindu, Buddhist and Christian features.

4 Hiran Minar
Just outside the city to the north, the odd-looking Hiran Minar is a beacon tower said to be built over the grave of Akbar's favourite elephant.

Hiran Minar

5 Pachisi Court
In the palace's main courtyard there is a giant outdoor board for *pachisi*, the original version of ludo. Akbar would play here using colourfully dressed servant girls as live pieces.

6 House of the Turkish Sultana
The "Turkish sultana" (one of Akbar's wives) probably didn't live in this little pleasure pavilion. More correctly, it is called the Anup Talao Pavilion, after the adjacent small square pool with a stage in the middle.

7 Daulat Khana
Akbar's private quarters have three parts. The library once housed his collection of over 25,000 manuscripts. The room behind it was his study, and upstairs was his bedroom, known as the *khwabgah*.

8 Panch Mahal
The "five-storey palace" narrows with each successive floor and marks the beginning of the *zenana* or women's quarters. Its columns originally had screens between them, shielding the women from view.

9 Sunehra Makan
Akbar's mother may have lived in the "golden house". Its interior murals, although sadly faded, are still impressive.

10 Jodhabai's Palace
The main harem was home to Akbar's senior wives (he had 13 wives in all). It is a grand affair, modelled on the ornate palaces of the Hindu Rajputs.

The Top 10 of Everything

A group of women praying at the shrine of Nizamuddin

🔟 Moments in History

The citadel of Qila Rai Pithora

① AD 736: Founding of Delhi

Delhi was founded by the Rajput Tomars in the Surajkund area, south of the modern city. In 1060, the town was relocated 10 km (6 miles) west by Tomar ruler Anangpal II, who created a new fortified citadel there called Lal Kot. Around 1160, the Tomars became vassals of the Chauhans, another Rajput clan from Ajmer, who extended Lal Kot and renamed it Qila Rai Pithora.

② 1192: Founding of the Delhi Sultanate

Muhammad of Ghori, from Ghazni (Afghanistan), invaded north India in 1191, but was defeated by Prithviraj Chauhan III at the Battle of Tarain. A year later, Muhammad returned, defeated Prithviraj and took control of northern India. He went home, leaving Qutbuddin Aibak, his general, in charge of Delhi. Aibak became the first sultan of Delhi following Muhammad Ghori's death in 1206.

③ 1327: To Daulatabad and Back Again

Muhammad bin Tughlaq moved the capital from Delhi to Daulatabad (present-day Devagiri), 1,500 km (932 miles) to the south. Delhi's entire population was forcibly relocated to the new city. Daulatabad, however, lasted only two years before Tughlaq abandoned it and returned to Delhi.

④ 1398: Invasion of Timur

A Mongol army led by Timur the Lame, or Tamerlaine as he is better known in the West, sacked Delhi and left it in ruins, leading to the fall of the Tughlaq Dynasty.

⑤ 1526: Arrival of the First Mughals

Babur, a Central Asian adventurer and former ruler of Fergana, Kabul and Samarkand, defeated the last Delhi sultan, Ibrahim Lodi, at the Battle of Panipat (1526) and ushered in the Mughal Dynasty.

Artwork depicting Babur in Kabul

⑥ 1638: Foundation of Shajahanabad

The fifth Mughal emperor, Shah Jahan, transferred India's capital from Agra (where it had been moved by his predecessor, Akbar) back to Delhi. Once there, he founded the brand new city of Shahjahanabad, or Old Delhi, as it is known today.

A depiction of the 1857 Uprising

7 1857: Indian Uprising

In 1857, Indian soldiers across north India revolted and seized control of major cities which were under British control, including Delhi, Lucknow and Kanpur. Delhi became the focus of the movement, as the sepoys rallied behind the Mughal emperor, Bahadur Shah Zafar II. The rebellion was quelled and the conflict stopped after months of bitter fighting. Not long afterwards, the city of Delhi was retaken by the British.

8 1911: Foundation of New Delhi

The capital of British India was moved from Calcutta to Delhi and work began on building the grandiose city of New Delhi under the creative leadership of Edwin Lutyens. The city was inaugurated in 1931 – ironically, the same year the British agreed, in principle, to grant India its independence at a future date.

9 1947: Independence

India was partitioned and became independent. Delhi lost a large proportion of its former Muslim population, while huge numbers of Hindu and Sikh refugees from Pakistan arrived in their place, decisively changing the city's cultural and demographic constitution.

10 1984: Assassination of Indira Gandhi

The assassination of Prime Minister Indira Gandhi (1917–84) by two of her Sikh bodyguards was followed by citywide rioting. Thousands of Sikhs were killed by lynch mobs and their homes were set on fire.

TOP 10 HISTORICAL FIGURES

1 Qutbuddin Aibak
The Turkish slave General Qutbuddin Aibak (1150–1210) faounded the Delhi Sultanate, which eventually saw 36 rulers from five separate dynasties control this region of north India.

2 Razia Sultan
Female sultan Razia (r. 1236–40) broke every gender stereotype of her time, appearing unveiled in public and going into battle on horseback.

3 Alauddin Khilji
Alauddin (r. 1296–1316) was perhaps the most brilliant – and certainly the most ruthless – of the Delhi sultans.

4 Muhammad bin Tughlaq
The second Tughlaq ruler (1300–51), was responsible for building the fourth city of Delhi, named Jahanpanah.

5 Sher Shah Suri
This formidable Afghan adventurer (1486–1545) wrested power from the second Mughal emperor, Humayun.

6 Shah Jahan
The sublime Taj Mahal was built by this Mughal emperor (1592–1666).

7 Bahadur Shah Zafar II
The last Mughal emperor, Bahadur Shah Zafar II (1775–1862), was the figurehead of the 1857 Uprising.

8 Mirza Ghalib
Ghalib (1797–1869) was the Urdu language's greatest poet, known particularly for his *ghazals (see p63)*.

9 Edwin Lutyens
This British architect (1869–1944) designed much of New Delhi.

10 Mohandas K Gandhi
The eminent leader (1869–1948) of the Indian independence movement was assassinated in Delhi.

Mohandas K Gandhi

🔟 Delhi Sultanate Sights

The modest Lal Gumbad tomb

① Lal Gumbad
MAP V2 ■ Panchsheel Park South, off Gamal Abdel Nasser Marg ■ Hauz Khas Metro ■ Open 24 hrs

Built for local Sufi saint Kabiruddin Aulia in 1397, the Lal Gumbad is very similar to the earlier tomb of Ghiyasuddin Tughlaq – a cube of red sandstone, almost devoid of extraneous decoration. This is Tughlaq architecture at its most austere.

② Hauz Khas
Hauz Khas or Green Park Metro

The lake in Hauz Khas was built by Alauddin Khilji in 1304 to supply water to his new city at Siri. Most of the pavilions around it were added half a century later by Feroz Shah Tughlaq, who is buried here.

③ Begumpuri Masjid
MAP V2 ■ Begumpur, off Guru Govind Singh Road ■ Hauz Khas Metro

The finest of the various Sultanate-era mosques

scattered about the city, the Begumpuri Masjid is a perfect example of the austere and monumental style favoured by the Tughlaq Dynasty. The simple mosque is raised, fortress-like, above the surrounding streets, centred on a huge courtyard, with a massive gateway above the central prayer hall.

④ Tomb of Ghiyasuddin Tughlaq
MAP X3 ■ Tughlaqabad ■ Tughlaqabad Metro

This simple, yet striking, red tomb is the final resting place of one of medieval India's most powerful rulers, Ghiyasuddin Tughlaq. The tomb is an almost windowless structure with sloping sides set within a small fortified compound.

⑤ Lodi Gardens
The delicately constructed octagonal tombs of Muhammad Shah, Sikander Lodi and other sultans are dotted throughout the idyllic Lodi Gardens *(see pp30–31)*. Their relatively small scale (and light style) illustrate the declining fortunes of the Sayyid and Lodi Dynasties.

⑥ Qutb Minar
The defining image of the Delhi Sultanate, the towering Qutb Minar *(see pp24–5)* is a perfect example of the simple, but grandiose, Sultanate architectural style, which was intended to symbolize both the military might of the new sultans from Afghanistan and the power of the then-newly arrived Islamic faith.

The lofty Qutb Minar

7 Khirki Masjid
MAP V3 ■ Press Enclave Road ■ Malviya Nagar Metro ■ Open sunrise–sunset daily

Another superbly atmospheric Tughlaq-era mosque that was built in the 1370s, the Khirki Masjid looks more like a labrynthine fortress than a peaceful place of worship.

8 Quwwat-ul-Islam
The oldest mosque in India, set in the Qutb complex (see p24), this is a fascinating study in cultural contrasts. The central courtyard, fashioned out of columns from Hindu and Jain temples that previously stood on this site, has a decidedly Hindu appearance. The magnificent screen of the prayer hall, however, is a classic work of Islamic architecture covered in Koranic inscriptions.

Ornate columns at Quwwat-ul-Islam

9 Tughlaqabad
Another monumental expression of the power of the Sultanate, the city of Tughlaqabad (see p101) was built by Ghiyasuddin Tughlaq, founder of the Tughlaq Dynasty. The massive fortified citadel – now largely in ruins – was built, astonishingly, in just two years.

10 Feroz Shah Kotla
All that remains of the great city of Ferozabad (see p88) is a walled enclosure containing the fragmentary remains of a royal palace, mosque and other structures. The most eye-catching feature here is the Ashokan column, which is perched atop the citadel and dates from the 3rd century BC.

TOP 10 DELHI SULTANS

1 Qutbuddin Aibak
The first Delhi sultan, Qutbuddin Aibak (1150–1210) founded the Delhi Sultanate's so-called Slave Dynasty.

2 Iltutmish
The son-in-law of Aibak, Iltutmish (r. 1211–36) extended the territory of the Sultanate from Punjab to Bengal.

3 Razia Sultan
Iltutmish's daughter (r. 1236–40) and India's only major female leader until Indira Gandhi, seven centuries later.

4 Alauddin Khilji
Alauddin (r. 1296–1316) was the most illustrious ruler of the Khilji Dynasty.

5 Ghiyasuddin Tughlaq
Ghiyasuddin Tughlaq (r. 1320–24) founded the Tughlaq Dynasty.

6 Muhammad bin Tughlaq
Eccentric ruler (r. 1325–51) who tried to relocate the capital from Delhi to Daulatabad but later moved it back.

7 Feroz Shah Tughlaq
Feroz Shah Tughlaq (r. 1351–88) tried to repair the damage inflicted on the Sultanate by his predecessor.

8 Khizr Khan
Khizr Khan (r. 1414–21) took advantage of the power vacuum created by Timur's invasion in 1398 to establish the Sayyid Dynasty (1414–51).

9 Buhlul Lodi
Punjab governor (r. 1451–89) who seized power from the Sayyids, establishing the last of the Sultanate's five dynasties, the Lodi Dynasty.

10 Sikander Lodi
Sikander Lodi (r. 1489–1517) was the last Delhi sultan. His son, Ibrahim Lodi (r. 1517–26), was overthrown by the great Babur, the first of the Mughals.

A depiction of Razia Sultan

TOP 10 Mughal Delhi Sights

Onion domes at Nizamuddin

1 Nizamuddin
The religious complex at Nizamuddin *(see pp94–5)* is home to several Mughal structures, including the tombs of Ataga Khan (1562) and the saint Nizamuddin Aulia (1325), both of which were built during the reign of Akbar.

2 Zinat ul Masjid
Dating from the reign of Aurangzeb, this neglected architectural gem is a perfect example of Mughal architecture in miniature – a scaled-down version of the Jama Masjid, with a trio of marbled onion domes sitting atop the beautifully proportioned and serene prayer hall below.

3 Humayun's Tomb
Humayun's Tomb *(see pp18–19)* exemplifies many of the design elements that were to become standard features of the Mughal style, including the use of red sandstone with marble inlay, enormous *iwans* and the setting of the entire tomb within a very pretty Persian-style *charbagh* garden.

4 Purana Qila
The oldest major Mughal monument in Delhi, the walled Purana Qila *(see p93)* was begun by Humayun and completed by his Afghan successor, Sher Shah Suri *(see p43)* after he had driven his rival into exile in Persia.

5 Khan-i-Khanan
The imposing tomb *(see p92)* of Abdur Rahim, who served as prime minister to Akbar, but later fell foul of Jahangir, is now dilapidated but still impressive. It is clearly modelled on the nearby Humayun's Tomb, though its rounded shape hints at the later Taj Mahal.

6 Jama Masjid
India's largest mosque, Shah Jahan's Jama Masjid *(see pp16–17)* is the epitome of Mughal religious architecture: a dramat-ically simple combination of massive arches, domes and slender minarets, towering above the streets of Old Delhi.

7 Zafar Mahal
Built by the Mughal emperor Akbar Shah II in the 18th century, and the last major monument of Mughal India, the Zafar Mahal *(see p27)*

Humayun's Tomb

summer palace is an exercise in architectural nostalgia by an increasingly powerless, and soon to be extinguished, dynasty.

⑧ Safdarjung's Tomb

The last major Mughal mausoleum in Delhi, Safdarjung's Tomb (see p94) is generally thought to exemplify the creative decline that set in following the demise of Shah Jahan, though its fanciful façades and interior lend it a certain kitsch charm entirely its own.

⑨ Red Fort

Despite suffering considerable damage during the 1857 Uprising and afterwards, the Red Fort (see pp12–13) remains a treasure trove of Mughal architectural styles, with grand gateways, formal gardens and a sequence of royal pavilions strung out along the ramparts.

The interior of Jamali-Kamali Masjid

⑩ Jamali-Kamali Masjid

Completed in 1536 during Humayun's first reign (see p19), the simple but elegant Jamali-Kamali Masjid (see p26) is Delhi's finest example of early-Mughal architecture.

TOP 10 MUGHAL DESIGN FEATURES

Floral pietra dura tilework

1 Pietra Dura
A hallmark of the Shah Jahan-era style, where colourful gemstones are embedded in white marble to create elaborate floral or abstract designs.

2 Iwans
Huge central arches providing a focus on the façades of tombs and mosques.

3 Cusped Arches
Staple of Mughal architecture, derived from Rajasthani and Bengali styles.

4 Red Sandstone and White Marble
A classic Mughal combination: façades of red sandstone that are decorated with bands of white marble inlay.

5 Jalis
Delicately carved marble or sandstone screens, often used to enclose tombs.

6 Tilework
A technique derived from Persia, using coloured tiles (usually, but not exclusively, blue) to decorate domes, window frames and façades.

7 Charbagh Gardens
Persian-style gardens, divided by water channels into four equal quadrants.

8 Domes
Distinctive Persian-style onion domes, often crowned with dramatic finials.

9 Chattris
Small, domed pavilions supported on four pillars, common in Hindu architecture and used on the eaves and minarets of Mughal buildings.

10 Jharokas
Distinctive balconied windows, richly carved – another classic feature adopted by the Mughals.

ᴛᴏᴘ10 Monuments of the 1857 Uprising

Muslims in the courtyard during daily prayer at Fatehpuri Masjid

1 Fatehpuri Masjid
This Chandni Chowk mosque (see p15) was a hotbed of religious fervour and nationalist sentiment during the 1857 Uprising. The British responded by sacking the mosque and selling it to a local businessman, although two decades later they bought it back and returned it to Delhi's Muslim community. A number of Indian soldiers killed in the uprising lie buried in the courtyard.

2 Flagstaff Tower
MAP B4 ▪ Magazine Road, Northern Ridge ▪ Vidhan Sabha Metro
Built in 1828 as a British signalling post, the tower served as a shelter for dozens of civilians fleeing the city after the outbreak of hostilities during the 1857 Uprising.

f Flagstaff Tower

3 Mutiny Monument
MAP E1 ▪ Rani Jhansi Road ▪ Pul Bangash Metro
At the southern end of the Northern Ridge, this grandiose Gothic-style Victorian monument, built in 1863, commemorates the British soldiers (and "native" troops in British employ) killed during the uprising, with panels listing the names, ranks and numbers of military fatalities. An additional panel, added in 1972, offers an Indian perspective on the events described and is worth a look.

4 British Residency
MAP H2 ▪ Sham Nath Marg ▪ Kashmiri Gate Metro
The old Neo-Classical British Residency was built around the ruins of a Mughal library erected by Dara Shikoh (1615–59), son of Shah Jahan. It is now home to the Archaeology Department of the Guru Gobind Singh Indraprastha University.

5 Northern Ridge
North of Old Delhi, the northern extension of the Aravalli Range forms a long, low ridge. This is where the refugees from Delhi converged during the 1857 Uprising, and where British forces gathered before launching an assault to recapture the city.

6 St James' Church

This beautiful Colonial-era church (see p85) holds a number of memorials to British civilians killed in Delhi during the 1857 Uprising. It also contains a memorial to the Reverend Midgeley John Jennings, then chaplain of Delhi, whose rather high-handed Christian evangelizing did much to enflame local religious sensibilities, and who was killed in the Red Fort during the first few hours of the revolt.

7 Magazine

MAP H2 ■ Sham Nath Marg
■ Kashmiri Gate Metro

Now marooned on a traffic island, this small British magazine was at the heart of the first day of fighting in Delhi. Surrounded by enemy Indian sepoys, the British troops stationed inside the magazine decided to blow it up rather than allow its stock of arms and ammunition to fall into Indian hands. The explosion killed around 400 sepoys and onlookers.

8 Kashmiri Gate

MAP G2 ■ Sham Nath Marg
■ Kashmiri Gate Metro

Now dwarfed by the vast new Kashmiri Gate Metro, this modest little Mughal-era gateway witnessed the most bitter fighting of the entire uprising, when British troops stormed the gate in order to force a route into the rebel-held city. A plaque at the rear commemorates those who were killed in the assault.

The Lal Darwaza or Bloody Gate

9 Lal Darwaza

MAP H6 ■ Mathura Road
■ Pragati Maidan Metro

The red sandstone Lal Darwaza (also known as the Khooni Darwaza, or Bloody Gate) marks the site of one of the most notorious episodes of the uprising (see p43), when British officer William Hodson summarily executed Mirza Mughal, Kizr Sultan and Abu Bakr, sons and grandson, respectively, of the last Mughal emperor.

10 Nicholson's Cemetery

Tucked away in Old Delhi, this atmospheric and rambling Colonial-era cemetery (see p88) is a haven from the chaotic hustle and bustle of the old city. Beautifully restored in 2006, it is the final resting place of hundreds of India's early European inhabitants. Of its many graves, monuments and tombs, the most famous is that of Brigadier-General John Nicholson (1822–57), a prominent British army commander and one of the key figures in the history of the 1857 Uprising – he is best known for planning and leading the final British assault on Delhi. Nicholson was killed in September 1857 during the bitter fighting that took place for the recapture of the city.

🔟 Cities of Delhi, Old and New

2 Lal Kot and Qila Rai Pithora

The first of Delhi's traditional seven cities, Lal Kot was established by a Rajput clan, the Tomars, in 1060. A century later, they became vassals of the Chauhans, who extended Lal Kot and renamed it Qila Rai Pithora. Both settlements were largely buried under the Qutb Minar *(see pp24–5)* complex.

3 Siri
MAP V2

The second city of Delhi, Siri was built during the reign of Alauddin Khilji *(see p43)*. These days little remains of it, barring a few sections of the walls. More impressive is the water tank Alauddin built nearby at Hauz Khas *(see p100)* to supply water to Siri. It was later expanded by Feroz Shah Tughlaq (r. 1351–88).

1 Indraprastha

The legendary city of Indraprastha, home of the Pandava brothers of the epic *Mahabharata*, is said to have stood on the site that is now occupied by the Purana Qila. Conclusive evidence is sadly lacking, although finds have been unearthed here dating to the 3rd century BC, and an ancient village stood here until the early 20th century. Today this is home to one of the oldest forts in Delhi and is a great place to visit.

4 Tuqhlaqabad

Built during the reign of Ghiyasuddin Tughlaq (r. 1320–24), Tuqhlaqabad *(see p101)*, the third city of Delhi, was quickly abandoned. The city's most impressive features are the massive fortified citadel and ramparts, stretching for over 6 km (4 miles), and the distinctive tomb of Ghiyasuddin himself. A smaller subsidiary fortress, known as Adilabad, stands nearby.

The ancient ruined citadel and ramparts of Tuqhlaqabad

**The buildings of the
Central Secretariat
in New Delhi**

5 Jahanpanah

Delhi's fourth city, Jahanpanah, was built by Muhammad bin Tughlaq *(see p43)* shortly before the eccentric ruler briefly abandoned Delhi for the city of Daulatabad. Two important monuments survive here: the Bijay Mandal, which is thought to be Tughlaq's palace, as well as the Bogumpuri Mosque *(see p100)*.

6 Ferozabad

Constructed by Feroz Shah Tughlaq, Ferozabad was the fifth city of Delhi. Today, the principal surviving structure is the walled palace known as Feroz Shah Kotla *(see p88)*, its crumbling remains topped by one of the city's two Ashokan pillars *(see p88)*.

7 Purana Qila

Built on the fabled site of Indraprastha, Purana Qila – the sixth city of Delhi – was begun by the second Mughal emperor Humayun *(see p19)* and completed by his great rival Sher Shah Suri *(see p43)*. Following Suri's death, Humayun reclaimed the Purana Qila *(see p93)*, but died within a year after falling down a steep flight of steps.

8 Shahjahanabad

Begun by Shah Jahan in 1638, Shahjahanabad (Old Delhi) was the last of Delhi's so-called seven cities. It was intended to provide North India with a capital to replace Agra.

9 New Delhi

Built in 1911–1931, the city of New Delhi was an attempt by the British to assert their Imperial credentials, featuring showpiece architectural landmarks including the Secretariat Buildings and the Rashtrapati Bhavan *(see p21)*. Edwin Lutyens was asked to create a city that would rival the great cities of the Mughals and the Delhi sultans and legitimize Britain's increasingly shaky hold on the country.

10 Satellite Cities

Thanks to the metro, Delhi's satellite towns have become more accessible and are attracting corporations and wealthy residents. To the south, Gurugram (formerly Gurgaon) is a city of gleaming high-rises, many the headquarters of IT companies. Noida in the east, is another shiny steel-and-glass IT hub.

The town of Gurugram at night

🔟 Places of Worship

The Baha'i Temple, popularly known as the Lotus Temple

1 Baha'i Temple

India's answer to the Sydney Opera House, this remarkable building *(see p99)* – an abstract composition inspired by the shape of an unfurling lotus flower – was built in 1986 by the Baha'is and is open to everyone. Founded by 19th-century Persian visionary Baha'u'llah, the Baha'i faith stresses the links between the major world religions and has over five million followers worldwide.

The Colonial-style St James' Church

2 St James' Church

Possibly the city's most attractive church *(see p85)*, this Colonial gem was built by the legendary Anglo-Indian soldier James Skinner (1778–1841). Barred from serving in the British army owing to his mixed race, Skinner established his own irregular cavalry regiment, Skinner's Horse, which still forms part of the Indian army to this day.

3 Gurudwara Bangla Sahib

Built in 1783 in honour of the eighth Sikh Guru Har Krishan, this *(see p80)* is the city's largest Sikh temple. The guru visited Delhi in 1664 during a cholera and smallpox epidemic, tending to the sick and offering them fresh water from the *sarovar* (lake) on the site, which is still believed to possess medicinal properties.

4 Zinat ul Masjid

Popularly known as the Ghata (Cloud) Masjid *(see p86)*, this beautiful building was commissioned by Aurangzeb's daughter Zinat ul Nisa and was completed in 1707. It is the only one of the city's later Mughal monuments grand enough to rival the earlier creations of Shah Jahan.

5 Lakshmi Narayan Mandir

This eye-catching Hindu temple *(see p79)*, popularly known as Birla Mandir, was commissioned by industrialist B D Birla and consecrated in 1939 by Gandhi – one of the first temples in India open to everyone, irrespective of caste. The spacious interior is centred on a shrine to Lakshmi and her consort Narayan (Vishnu), flanked by images of Durga and Shiva.

6 Nizamuddin

One of the most magical places in Delhi, the wonderfully atmospheric religious complex of Nizamuddin *(see p94)* grew up around the revered *dargah* (Muslim shrine) of the Chishti Sufi saint Nizamuddin Auliya. Among the cluster of structures now surrounding the saint's tomb are the Jamat Khana Masjid (1325) and the graves of the famous poet Amir Khusrau (1253–1325) and Princess Jahanara, Shah Jahan's daughter.

7 Lal Mandir
This Jain temple *(see p14)* is one of the city's most important. Topped by a cluster of towers, made of red Kota stone, it has a richly painted interior, full of diminutive marble images of various Jain gurus in glass cases. Next to the temple is a small "bird hospital", where birds are fed and cared for – evidence of the profound respect that the Jain religion has for all forms of life.

Visitors at Akshardham Temple

8 Akshardham Temple
This gargantuan modern Hindu temple *(see p94)*, inaugurated in 2005, was built in honour of the sage Bhagwan Shri Swaminarayan (1781–1830), who left his birthplace in Uttar Pradesh at the age of 11 and walked for seven years and 12,000 km (7,456 miles) before establishing an ashram in Gujarat. From here, he preached a message of non-violence and spiritual unity, attracting many Hindu followers as well as Muslim and Zoroastrian devotees.

Jama Masjid, India's largest mosque

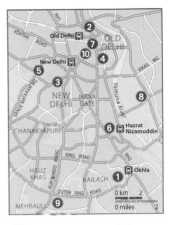

9 Begumpuri Masjid
Built in the 1340s by Muhammad bin Tughlaq as part of his city of Jahanpanah, this little-visited but atmospheric mosque *(see p100)* is one of the finest in Delhi. The mosque is centred on a huge courtyard surrounded by domed arcades, with a fortress-like gateway leading into the prayer hall – a perfect example of Tughlaq architecture at its rugged and imposing best.

10 Jama Masjid
Despite the exodus of many of the old city's Muslims during the Partition in 1947, Delhi's spectacular Jama Masjid *(see pp16–17)* remains a key centre for Islamic worship.

🔟 Museums and Galleries

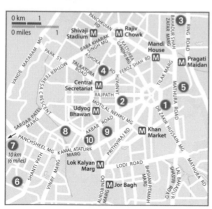

4 National Philatelic Museum

Heaven for stamp enthusiasts, the National Philatelic Museum (see p80) holds a copy of every Indian stamp produced since Independence (around 1,700 issues), as well as an interesting selection of international stamps and the personal belongings of a mid-19th-century postman.

5 Crafts Museum

This museum (see pp28–9) is another of Delhi's must-see cultural attractions, showcasing a variety of artifacts inspired by the country's indigenous folk-art traditions. Exhibits include detailed ivory carvings, as well as a vast collection of textiles and fabrics and Hindu bronzes, while outside in the grounds you can see a set of traditional buildings from all around India.

1 National Gallery of Modern Art (NGMA)

Located in a purpose-built structure, the National Gallery of Modern Art (see p80) houses works dating from 1857 to the present. Among them are a good selection of miniatures, East India Company Art and works by classic Orientalist artists such as Thomas Daniell, plus a collection of works by the Bengali artist Nandalal Bose.

2 National Museum

The National Museum (see pp32–5) is an obligatory stop on any tour of Delhi's museums. It has a superb array of exhibits covering every epoch in the country's history, ranging from priceless Harappan artifacts through to Chola bronzes and Mughal miniatures.

3 National Gandhi Museum

The city's second Gandhi museum (see p88) is close to Raj Ghat where the body of Father of the Nation was cremated. Exhibits on display include Gandhi's memorabilia and that of his wife, plus six telephones on which visitors can listen to his famous speeches in Hindi and English.

6 National Rail Museum

India's love affair with the railway is celebrated in this fine museum (see p95) containing assorted antique steam engines and opulent carriages, including those once belonging to the maharajas of Mysore and Baroda, and the Prince of Wales.

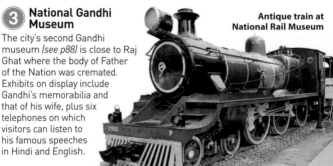

Antique train at National Rail Museum

Gandhi Smriti, where Gandhi spent the last days of his life

7 Sulabh International Museum of Toilets

MAP A5 ■ Mahavir Enclave, Palam Dabri Marg ■ 2503 1518 ■ Uttam Nagar East Metro ■ Open 10am–5pm Mon–Sat ■ www.sulabh toiletmuseum.org

Although this museum may sound like a joke, it has quite a serious purpose, being part of the neo-Gandhian Sulabh International Movement, which aims to promote public hygiene, with many displays on lavatorial habits.

Sulabh International Museum of Toilets

8 Jawaharlal Nehru Memorial Museum

Teen Murti House, formerly called Flagstaff House, was built in 1930 as the residence of the British military commander-in-chief and later became home to India's first Prime Minister Jawaharlal Nehru (1889–1964). There's a library, and a few photographs and newspaper cuttings on display, but the main attraction is the house (see p80) itself, including rooms left exactly as they were when Nehru lived here.

9 Gandhi Smriti

Formerly known as Birla House, this Neo-Classical mansion (see p79) is where Gandhi (1869–1948) spent the last 144 days of his life. Displays include a touching collection of the Mahatma's personal belongings, such as the watch he was wearing when he was assasinated, which stopped at the moment of his death.

10 Indira Gandhi Memorial Museum

This museum (see p78) is the former home of Prime Minister Indira Gandhi (1917–84), who was assassinated in the garden here by two of her Sikh bodyguards. The absorbing exhibits include personal belongings and photos, plus a section devoted to her son Rajiv (1944–91), including the shoes he was wearing when he was killed by Tamil separatists in 1991.

Exhibits at Indira Gandhi Memorial

TOP 10 Delhi-Inspired Books

Indian author Anita Desai

The Indian Express, offers some fascinating insights into the city's complex social fabric, from the lives of local slum dwellers to the Westernized airs of Delhi's high-flying aristocratic elite.

1 Clear Light of Day (Anita Desai)

This is Anita Desai's most obviously autobiographical work, centred on the contrasting stories of two sisters from Old Delhi – one of whom leaves the city and the other of whom remains – and their subsequent reunion.

2 The White Tiger (Aravind Adiga)

A Booker Prize-winning debut novel by Chennai-born Aravind Adiga, this is partly set in Delhi, and relates the murderous career of anti-hero Balram Halwai, with insights into contemporary Indian society en route.

Delhi: Adventures in a Megacity

3 Scoop-wallah: Life On a Delhi Daily (Justine Hardy)

This engrossing account of a year spent by English journalist Justine Hardy as a reporter for

4 Trees of Delhi: A Field Guide (Pradip Krishen)

With a total ban on high-rise constructions still effective across large parts of the capital, Delhi's skyline is dominated not just by buildings but by trees. Ecologist and tree-lover Pradip Krishen's field guide provides an excellent introduction to some of the common varieties of trees that dot the city which, by many accounts, has become greener over recent years.

5 The Delhi Omnibus (introduction by Narayani Gupta)

This omnibus captures not just the physical history of the city, but the manner in which the people have invented and reinvented themselves over time. It contains writings by Percival Spear, Narayani Gupta, R E Frykenberg and Christopher Bayly.

6 Delhi: Adventures in a Megacity (Sam Miller)

This very entertaining eye-witness account of contemporary Delhi follows a spiralling per-ambulation through the city, from the centre of Connaught Place out into the suburbs, with wonderfully evocative descriptions of the many people and places encountered on the journey.

7 Delhi: A Novel (Khushwant Singh)

This is an engaging novel by one of India's foremost modern writers.

Historical snapshots of the city through the ages – culminating in the anti-Sikh riots of 1984 – are interspersed with a secondary narrative about a journalist and the passionate relationship he develops with a *hijra* (eunuch).

(8) City of Djinns (William Dalrymple)

A beautifully written portrait of Delhi's multilayered personality, this book is particularly strong on the city's history, interspersed with richly comic snapshots of the modern city.

(9) Twilight in Delhi (Ahmed Ali)

A novel by Delhi-born Ahmed Ali, this paints a beautiful portrait of the city at the beginning of the 20th century – an elegiac lament for the city's rapidly disappearing Mughal traditions in the face of the Colonial and European cultural onslaught.

(10) The Last Mughal (William Dalrymple)

A landmark study of the 1857 Uprising, drawing on unpublished contemporary source. This is the most even-handed account of the conflict yet published in English.

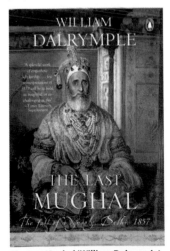

The Last Mughal **(William Dalrymple)**

TOP 10 FILMS BASED IN DELHI

Poster art for *Monsoon Wedding*

1 Fire (1996)
A controversial tale of a lesbian affair between two Delhi housewives.

2 Monsoon Wedding (2001)
Mira Nair's marvellously evocative portrait of the people and places of contemporary Delhi, combining social comedy with stunning cinematography.

3 Rang De Basanti (2006)
An influential film by director Rakeysh Omprakash Mehra about five young men who are trying to expose India's widespread political corruption.

4 Khosla Ka Ghosla! (2006)
A comedy drama depicting the battle between a middle-class family and a real estate shark over a plot of land.

5 Oye Lucky! Lucky Oye! (2008)
A comedy with Abhay Deol playing a "super thief" alongside a lovable host of rather disreputable characters.

6 Delhi-6 (2009)
A Rakeysh Omprakash Mehra film depicting the lives and loves of an eclectic array of Old Delhi characters.

7 Dev.D (2009)
Clever, contemporary reworking of the classic Bengali movie *Devdas*.

8 Band Baajaa Baraat (2010)
A refreshing love story following the ups and downs of two rival wedding planners in modern Delhi.

9 Delhi Belly (2011)
A black comedy, starring Imran Khan, about three friends who share a room in Delhi and somehow get involved in an underworld crime plot.

10 Vicky Donor (2012)
Reflecting a city coming to grips with modernity, with Ayushmann Khurrana as a Punjabi sperm donor who falls in love with a wordly Bengali banker.

🔟 Parks and Gardens

Statue at Buddha Jayanti Park

English styles, they have many rare species of flora, including 250 types of roses and 60 types of bougainvilleas.

4 Hauz Khas Deer Park
Close to the old tank and monuments of Hauz Khas Village (see p100), the Hauz Khas Deer Park is an area of peaceful, shady woodland, complete with bounding spotted deer, peacocks and abundant bird life.

5 Qudsia Bagh
North of Old Delhi lies Qudsia Bagh (see p88), created in 1748 as a royal pleasure park by Qudsia Begum (1801–81), wife of Mughal emperor Muhammad Shah. Little survives of the park's original buildings apart from a florid gateway, and a delicate little mosque situated at the garden's most southeastern end.

1 Buddha Jayanti Park
MAP K2 ■ Vandemataram Marg ■ Jhandewalan Metro ■ Open 5am–7pm daily

Hemmed in amidst the woodland of the Ridge west of New Delhi, this beautiful park was created in 1993 to mark the 2,500th anniversary of the Buddha's enlightenment. A Buddha statue sits within the park.

2 Lodi Gardens
Arguably the most attractive gardens (see pp30–31) in Delhi, with idyllic lawns and shady patches of woodland dotted with the imposing tombs of assorted Lodi and Sayyid rulers and nobles.

3 Mughal Gardens
Tucked away in the grounds of Rashtrapati Bhavan, the Mughal Gardens (see p21) are open to the public only for a month in spring, but are worth a visit. Designed by Edwin Lutyens in a blend of Mughal and

6 Talkatora Gardens
MAP L2 ■ Mother Teresa Crescent ■ Open sunrise–sunset daily

Behind Rashtrapati Bhavan, these 18th-century gardens are among central Delhi's most popular parks. They are prettiest in spring when the colourful shrubs burst into life.

7 Garden of Five Senses
MAP V3 ■ Said-ul-Ajaib village, near Mahavirsthal on the Mehrauli–Badarpur Road ■ Saket Metro ■ Open Apr–Sep: 9am–7pm daily (Oct–Mar: until 6pm) ■ Adm

This is Delhi's most artistic garden, dotted with sculptures. The gardens themselves are divided into differently landscaped areas, with sensory themes and names such as the "Trail of Fragrance" and "Colour Gardens".

(8) Nehru Park
MAP L6 ▪ **Panchsheel Road, Chanyakapuri** ▪ **Open 5am–8pm daily**

Nehru Park is one of the most popular retreats in South Delhi, with spacious lawns, a pool and an open-air gym with fitness equipment. The park frequently hosts concerts.

(9) Raj Ghat
These gardens *(see p85)* are best known as the place where the funeral rites of modern India's most important leaders took place, including Mahatma Gandhi, Indira Gandhi, Rajiv Gandhi and Jawaharlal Nehru, each of whom is commemorated with a monument.

Mahatma Gandhi memorial, Raj Ghat

(10) Coronation Park
MAP B4 ▪ **Shanti Swaroop Tyagi Marg, near Nirankari Sarovar** ▪ **Open sunrise–sunset daily**

Some 19 km (12 miles) north of Connaught Place, this was the site of the three British Durbars of 1887, 1903 and 1911. After independence, the park was used as a dumping ground for Raj-era statues, including a statue of King George V that once stood in front of India Gate.

The Mughal Gardens

TOP 10 INDIAN TREES

The flowers of the gulmohar tree

1 Gulmohar (*Delonix regia*)
The Indian flame tree has distinctive fern-like leaves and bright red flowers.

2 Neeli Gulmohar (*Jacaranda mimosifolia*)
The jacaranda is a flowering tree, which explodes in spring into a very distinctive purple-blue blossom.

3 Peepul (*Ficus religiosa*)
A species of banyan fig, this is also Buddhism's sacred tree (commonly known as the bodhi tree).

4 Amaltas (*Cassia fistula*)
A shrub (Indian laburnum in English) with Ayurvedic properties, this bursts into cascading yellow flowers in spring.

5 Champa (*Plumeria rubra*)
A species of frangipani, this is one of the most common Indian flowering shrubs, producing huge white blooms.

6 Semal (*Bombax ceiba*)
The red silk cotton tree is an attractive ornamental tree and especially pretty in spring, when it is covered in vibrant red flowers, with no leaves.

7 Jamun (*Syzygium cumini*)
The evergreen black plum is known for its large purple berries. It also features in the epic, the *Ramayana*.

8 Kachnar (*Bauhinia variegata*)
The popular ornamental orchid tree has scented pink or white flowers.

9 Dhak (*Butea monosperma*)
This pretty flowering species, known as the flame of the forest in English, has curved, bright orange flowers.

10 Neem (*Azadirachta indica*)
A common South Asian tree (Indian lilac), the neem is renowned for its medicinal properties, hence its popular description as the "village pharmacy".

🔟 Off the Beaten Track

① Shankar's International Dolls Museum

MAP H6 ■ 4 Bahadur Shah Zafar Marg ■ 2331 6970 ■ Open 10am–6pm Tue–Sun (last entry 5:30pm) ■ Adm ■ www.childrensbooktrust.com/dollsmuseum.html

Doll enthusiasts will love this prodigious collection of over 6,000 dolls from around the world, many dressed in regional and national costumes, and including amusing mannequins of John Wayne, Louis Armstrong and Henry VIII.

② Majnu ka Tila

MAP B4 ■ Aruna Nagar, Outer Ring Road ■ 15 min walk or short auto-rickshaw ride from Vidhan Sabha Metro

Here in Delhi's little Tibet the Dalai Lama's image beams down from the wall of almost every establishment. Visitors can purchase prayer wheels, thangkas (traditional Buddhist religious paintings) and books about Tibet and enjoy excellent Tibetan food.

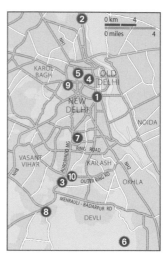

Prayer wheels, Majnu ka Tila

③ Adhchini

MAP V2 ■ Qutab Enclave, Aurobindo Marg ■ Hauz Khas Metro

An urban village, with residents, who mainly belong to an ethnic group called the Jats, Adhchini contains a 16th-century Lodi mosque and an impressive shrine to the mother of Nizamuddin Auliya (see p94).

④ Kalan Masjid

MAP G5 ■ In an alley opposite 2063 Mohammed Deen Haichi Marg

Built in 1387 and older than Old Delhi itself, this blue-and-green mosque, located near Turkman Gate, was – along with Khirki Masjid (see p45) – one of seven mosques commissioned by Feroz Shah's chief minister Khan-i-Jahan Junan Shah. It is the only one still in use today.

⑤ Masjid Mubarak Begum

MAP G4 ■ 4959 Hauz Razi, Lalkuan Bazaar Road ■ Chawri Bazaar Metro

This charming private mosque was built in 1823 for the Indian wife of Sir David Ochterlony, British Resident at the Mughal Court. Hidden away above a busy bazaar, and accessed by a narrow stairway between two shops (guests must take their shoes off at the top), it has a tiny prayer hall with only enough room for ten worshippers.

6 Surajkund Dam
Anangpur, 20 km (12 miles)
S of central Delhi, 4 km (2 miles)
W of NHPC Chowk metro station
■ Surajkund Tank: open sunrise–
sunset daily ■ Adm

Way off the beaten track, but still
within easy reach of the metro, this
is Delhi's very oldest construction,
built under the Tomar king Anangpal
in the 8th century to store rainwater
for irrigation. Surajkund Tank, 2 km
(1 mile) to its north, is an ancient
10th-century reservoir, which was
also built under the Tomars.

7 Aliganj
MAP N7 ■ Between Aliganj
Road and Karbala Road, Jor Bagh
■ Jor Bagh Metro ■ www.
shahemardan.org

Once the estate of the Shiite rulers
of Awadh, the family of the Nawab of
Safdarjung, this area has interesting
18th-century buildings. Most notable
among these is the Shah-e-Mardan
Dargah, a Shia shrine where Sunnis
and some Hindus go to pray.

8 Chhattarpur Mandir
MAP B7 ■ Main Chhattarpur
Road ■ 2680 2925 ■ Chhattarpur
Metro ■ Open 6am–10pm daily

This was the biggest temple in India
when it was built in 1974, but it is
really a park-like compound with
several temples inside it, presided
over by a 30-m (98-ft) high statue
of the monkey god, Hanuman. The
complex was financed by followers
of a guru known as Babaji, whose
ashes rest in one of the temples.

Paharganj Christian Cemetery

9 Paharganj Christian Cemetery
MAP E5 ■ Ramdwara Road, Nehru
Bazaar ■ 2358 5710 ■ Open daily

It is easy to forget that Christianity
is an important religion in India,
where three states still have Christian
majorities. This little cemetery has
faithfully served Delhi's Christian
community since the 19th century,
but really comes to life on Halloween,
when it sparkles with candles left
by relatives visiting the deceased.

10 Bijay Mandal
MAP V2 ■ Kalu Sarai, near
Hauz Khas Metro

Around 100 m (330 ft) north of
Begumpuri Masjid (see p100), this
sturdy but atmospheric ruin is all that
remains of Sultan Muhammad bin
Tughlaq's palace. Visitors can climb
to the octagonal pavilion on its roof
for great views over the city.

The Chhattarpur Mandir complex

TOP10 Performing Arts Venues

Classical dance performance during a show at Kamani Auditorium

1 Kamani Auditorium
MAP Q1 ■ Mandi House,
1 Copernicus Marg ■ 4350 3351
■ Mandi House Metro ■ www.
kamaniauditorium.org

The Kamani Auditorium is one of the city's leading venues for classical music and dance, attracting leading performers from across the country.

2 Triveni Kala Sangam
MAP G7 ■ 205 Tansen
Marg ■ 2371 8833 ■ Mandi
House Metro

This cultural centre houses a range of venues, including galleries, an auditorium and an open-air theatre, which stages regular music and dance performances.

3 Shri Ram Centre for Performing Arts
MAP Q1 ■ 4 Safdar Hashmi
Marg ■ 2371 4307 ■ Mandi
House Metro ■ www.shriram
centre.org

Established in 1975, this is an important theatrical venue, with its own outstanding repertory company, staging a wide range of interesting productions that include musical, traditional and experimental theatre.

4 Sangeet Natak Akademi
MAP P1 ■ Rabindra Bhavan,
35 Feroz Shah Road ■ 2338 7246
■ Mandi House Metro ■ www.
sangeetnatak.org

This is one of the country's foremost performing arts venues, and home to Delhi's finest open-air theatre. It also has a library and a gallery featuring a range of traditional musical instruments, masks and puppets.

5 National School of Drama (NSD)
MAP Q1 ■ Bahawalpur
House, 1 Bhagwan Das Road
■ 2338 9402 ■ Mandi House
Metro ■ www.nsd.gov.in

The National School of Drama (NSD) is the country's leading academy for aspiring actors. The productions are staged by current students and the school's professional repertory company.

Theatre artist at NSD

6 Parsi Anjuman Hall
MAP H5 ■ Bahadur Shah
Zafar Marg ■ 2323 8615 ■ Pragati
Maidan Metro

Home to the Dances of India show (daily at 6:45pm), featuring a programme of classical and folk dances.

7 India International Centre

MAP P6 ■ 40 Max Mueller Marg ■ 2461 9431 ■ www.iicdelhi.nic.in

Besides regular music, dance and theatrical performances, the India International Centre (IIC) hosts exhibitions and talks attracting leading cultural personalities such as Salman Rushdie and Noam Chomsky. It also hosts a popular cinema club with art-house film screenings.

8 Nizamuddin

The fascinating religious enclave of Nizamuddin *(see p94)* is Delhi's most atmospheric venue for impromptu music, with nightly performances of ecstatic *qawwali* singing around the shrine of Nizamuddin Auliya, the famous Sufi saint.

9 Siri Fort

MAP V2 ■ Khel Gaon Marg ■ 2649 3370 ■ Green Park Metro

The extensive Siri Fort Cultural Complex boasts three auditoriums (the largest seating almost 2,000 people), staging a range of big-name events, particularly Indian classical music concerts, dance and film.

10 India Habitat Centre (IHC)

MAP P6 ■ Lodi Road ■ 2468 2001/2009 ■ www.indiahabitat.org

This is one of Delhi's state-of-the-art performing-arts venues, and hosts regular music, dance and cultural events such as art-house film screenings and talks.

A literary festival at the IHC

A party of *qawwali* singers

TOP 10 FORMS OF INDIAN CLASSICAL MUSIC

1 Qawwali
Sufi devotional music, with ecstatic, rhythmic singing used by devotees to achieve the trance-like state that Sufis believe brings them closer to God.

2 Dhrupad
One of the oldest and most austere forms of Hindustani classical vocal music, said to have developed from the chanting of Vedic hymns.

3 Thumri
A type of love song, usually performed in Braj Bhasha, a dialect of Hindi.

4 Dadra
A light form of Hindustani classical vocal music popular in north India.

5 Tarana
North Indian vocal genre involving the rapid singing of musical syllables based on Persian/Arabic phonemes.

6 Kriti
The major vocal genre of Carnatic music, divided into three parts, and with a religious theme.

7 Varnam
Form of Carnatic vocal music designed to bring out the qualities of the underlying raga.

8 Padam
Light classical love songs in the Carnatic tradition, often sung during Bharatanatyam dance performances.

9 Ghazal
Persian-derived light classical song form, often using lyrics by Urdu poets.

10 Raga and Khayal
The system of modes underlying all Indian classical music, a framework for composition and improvisation. A *khayal* is the extended, improvised elaboration of a raga using a lyrical composition called a *bandish*.

Ⓣ⑩ Places to Eat

① Olive Bar & Kitchen
Located in the rustic yet swanky One Style Mile, Olive Bar & Kitchen *(see p105)* is one of the prettiest restaurants in town, with a lovely, airy courtyard and the Qutb Minar providing a stunning back-drop. The food here, mainly Mediterranean, Indian and Italian, is delicious too.

Indian Accent fusion cuisine

② SodaBottleOpenerWala
Straight out of Bombay but with a strong Iranian influence, this restaurant *(see p97)* specializes in the food of the Parsi community. As well as *dhansak*, there are more adventurous dishes such as sweet-and-sour *brinjal patio* or the berry *pulao*, made famous by Bombay's Britannia restaurant. Baked goodies include ginger biscuit and mawa cake.

③ Chor Bizarre
This place *(see p89)* specializes in excellent Kashmiri dishes rarely found elsewhere, such as *goshtaba* (slow-cooked mutton in yoghurt and cardamon) and a wonderful Kashmiri version of *dum aloo*. The decor is delightfully eccentric.

④ Indian Accent
A superb modern Indian fusion restaurant *(see p97)*, where the dishes run from paneer tikka quesadillas and tofu coriander vadas to tandoori bacon prawns. It can be difficult to make a decision with the range of innovative local dishes on offer so it's worth checking out the excellent vegetarian and non-vegetarian tasting menus on offer.

⑤ Saravana Bhavan
An excellent and inexpensive south Indian vegetarian restaurant *(see p83)*, where diners can feast on *idli sambar*, *masala dosa* and many other south Indian specialities, or tuck into a tasty vegetarian *thali*. If that is too filling, visitors can go for the mini tiffin, which offers a small taste of everything on the menu.

⑥ Spice Route
This elegant hotel restaurant *(see p83)* offers guests a special dining experience. The cuisine is from south-east Asia and the Indian state of Kerala – it is fiery, and the emphasis is on fish and seafood. A tasting menu is available in the evenings.

Diners lunching at the whimsically decorated Chor Bizarre

7 Wasabi By Morimoto

Dark wood sets the tone for this top-class Japanese restaurant *(see p83)*. After a drink at the exclusive sake bar, sample some steamed oysters followed by tenderloin *teppenyaki*. Round the meal off with a pungent, yet surprisingly cooling, serving of wasabi sorbet.

Table setting at Bukhara

8 Bukhara

With a guest list that includes former US President Bill Clinton, Bukhara *(see p97)* offers a rich menu that includes the city's best-loved dishes. The buttery *dal bukhara* (lentils) is legendary, as is the succulent, melt-in-the-mouth lamb dish and the *Sikandari raan*.

9 The China Kitchen

A far cry from the usual Indian-influenced Chinese fare served up in the city, the food in The China Kitchen *(see p105)* is modern and experimental yet still deeply rooted in traditional, primarily Szechuan, flavours. Diners swear the Peking Duck is the best in Delhi.

10 Karim's

Boasting a line of chefs that, apparently, used to prepare meals for Mughal emperors, Karim's *(see p89)* is arguably the city's most famous restaurant. Try the excellent mutton *korma* and *seekh kebabs*.

TOP 10 BARS AND NIGHTCLUBS

1 PCO
A "speakeasy" *(see p103)* boasting retro decor, a well-stocked bar and exotic cocktails. Requires a secret code – periodically changed – for entry.

2 Kitty Su
Colourful nightclub *(see p82)* off Connaught Place with a vibrant atmosphere and regular concerts and events.

3 1911
A quiet, elegant Art Deco place, 1911 *(see p82)* is steeped in old-world charm.

4 Rick's
Sample the many wines and cocktails at this urban lounge bar *(see p82)*.

5 Social
Offering all-day breakfast and signature drinks such as the *Aacharoska* (caipiroska with Indian lime pickle), this café-bar *(see p103)* is a must visit.

6 Monkey Bar
Fun and quirky, this Indian-inspired gastropub *(see p103)* serves up innovative dishes and cocktails.

7 Fio Cookhouse & Bar
Great thin-crust pizzas and potent cocktails with a twist are available here *(see p105)*.

8 G-Bar
MAP T2 ▪ The Grand, Nelson Mandela Marg ▪ 2677 1234 ▪ Open 6pm–3am daily
This bar attracts a young crowd with its lively music and upbeat atmosphere.

9 Cirrus 9
The Oberoi Hotel's rooftop bar *(see p103)* offers guests well-curated music, a wide selection of cocktails and magnificent views.

10 Aqua
An elegant spot for drinks, Aqua *(see p82)* has an iridescent pool, curtained pavilions and designer bar.

The elegant, alfresco Aqua

≛10 Bazaars of Old Delhi

① Dariba Kalan
MAP H3 ▪ Chandni Chowk ▪ Chandni Chowk Metro ▪ Open 11am–8pm Mon–Sat

Dating back to the days of Emperor Shah Jahan, "The Street of the Incomparable Pearl" is Old Delhi's foremost jewellery bazaar. The shops here sell an array of precious stones and metals including an especially good selection of silverware, as well as traditional attar-based *itr* perfumes.

② Ballimaran
MAP G3 ▪ Chandni Chowk ▪ Chandni Chowk Metro ▪ Open 11am–8pm Mon–Sat

The Chandni Chowk end of this long Old Delhi thoroughfare is the place to go to for shoes and slippers.

Dry fruits on sale at Khari Baoli

③ Khari Baoli
MAP F3 ▪ Chandni Chowk ▪ Chandni Chowk Metro ▪ Open 11am–8pm Mon–Sat

Said to be the biggest spice market in Asia, Khari Baoli is one of Old Delhi's most absorbing sights. Lively and congested in equal measure, it is lined with shops crammed full of all kinds of spices, pulses, dried fruits and other cooking ingredients.

The crowded stalls of Kinari Bazaar

④ Kinari Bazaar
MAP G3 ▪ Chandni Chowk ▪ Chandni Chowk Metro ▪ Open 11am–8pm Mon–Sat

Just off Dariba Kalan, the shops of Kinari Bazaar are famous for their wedding paraphernalia and other "fancy goods" – garlands of fake flowers and banknotes, reams of gold and silver tinsel, bridal veils, turbans for grooms and sparkly costume jewellery. They also sell items used in the *Ramayana* performances that are staged all over the city during the festival of Dussehra.

⑤ Guliyan Bazaar
MAP G4 ▪ Chawri Bazaar Metro

Stretching around the northwestern side of Jama Masjid, this is the place to come to stock up on fireworks for a wedding or a festival, with shops filled with piles of brightly coloured boxes full of rockets, firecrackers and other things that go bang.

⑥ Nai Sarak
MAP G4 ▪ Chawri Bazaar Metro

This street, created by the British in 1857 (hence the name, meaning "New Street"), cuts across the heart of the old city. It is now Old Delhi's main book market, with small shops selling dog-eared, second-hand school and college textbooks.

7 Car Parts Bazaar
MAP G4 ■ Chawri Bazaar Metro

Sprawling around the south and west sides of the Jama Masjid, this is one of Old Delhi's more workaday bazaars selling mechanical bits and bobs. Visitors will find everything from wheels, doors, hubcaps, panels and entire engines – a surreal sight in the shadow of the beautiful mosque.

8 Katra Neel
MAP G3 ■ Chandni Chowk ■ Chandni Chowk Metro ■ Open 11am–8pm Mon–Sat

Just off Chandni Chowk, this fascinating labyrinth of tiny alleyways is cluttered with shops selling all manner of ladies' clothing – shawls, salwar kameezes, saris – and a wide variety of textiles, such as brocades from Benarasi, silk and voile.

9 Chawri Bazaar
MAP G4 ■ Chawri Bazaar Metro

Old Delhi's stationery bazaar is devoted to writing paper, greetings cards and other paper products. Paper here is sold by weight and is very cheap. Shops at the western end of the road specialize in lovely brass and copper ornaments.

10 Meena Bazaar
On the steps around the Jama Masjid is Old Delhi's religious bazaar (see p16), with stalls selling prayer rugs, Koranic inscriptions, pictures of Mecca and Islamic-style clocks.

A shoe stall at Meena Bazaar

TOP 10 SHOPS AND MARKETS

Colourful handicrafts at Dilli Haat

1 Dilli Haat
A range of Indian craft items (see p96).

2 State Emporia Complex
MAP F7 ■ A–5 Baba Kharak Singh Marg
A must-visit for anyone interested in India's rich arts and crafts heritage.

3 Janpath Market
MAP F7 ■ Janpath ■ Open daily
Everything from export-reject clothes to pretty handmade paper lanterns.

4 Khan Market
MAP P5 ■ Open 10am–7:30pm Mon–Sat
Chic shops and restaurants, plus smaller shops selling lovely trinkets.

5 Santushti
Panchsheel Marg, Chanakyapuri ■ Open 10am–8pm daily
Classy shopping complex selling an assortment of beautiful designerwear.

6 Connaught Place
Elegant Georgian-style crescents housing Delhi's most important commercial space (see p77).

7 Hauz Khas Village
MAP U2 ■ Hauz Khas Village ■ Open 10am–8:30pm Mon–Sat
Lovely art galleries, cafés and shops.

8 Sarojini Nagar
MAP V1 ■ Sarojini Nagar ■ Open 10am–8:30pm Tue–Sun
Cheap heaps of export-reject clothes.

9 Daryaganj Sunday Book Market
MAP H5 ■ Open 7am–7pm Sun
A huge market for cheap second-hand books, most in English.

10 Select Citywalk Complex
MAP V3 ■ A-3 District Centre Saket ■ 4211 4211 ■ Open 10am–11pm daily
Luxurious mall with stores offering major international brand names.

🔟 Delhi for Free

The fascinating ruins at Mehrauli Archaeological Park

1 Mehrauli Archaeological Park

With over 70 monuments, including tombs, mosques, gateways and step-wells, from every century between the 13th and the 19th, this extensive park *(see p100)* is full of interesting sights and is also free to visit.

2 Films and Concerts

Alliance Française: 72 K K Birla Marg, Lodi Estate; delhi.afindia.org ▪ American Center: 24 Kasturba Gandhi Marg; in.usembassy.gov

Cultural centres such as the American Center and the Alliance Française often host free movies, concerts and other events, although visitors may have to register or get passes in advance. The National Gandhi Museum *(see p54)* puts on free films about Gandhi's life (in English on Saturdays at 4pm).

3 Museums for Free

National Gallery of Modern Art: Guided walks at 11am, 1:30pm & 3:30pm

Not far from one another, the Indira Gandhi Memorial Museum *(see p78)*, the Jawaharlal Nehru Memorial Museum *(see p80)* and Gandhi Smriti *(see p79)* are all free. While there is an admission charge to enter the National Gallery of Modern Art *(see p80)*, the museum organises a series of guided walks, which take you around the exhibitions on display at no extra cost. Other free museums include the National Gandhi Museum *(see p54)*, the

National Philatelic Museum *(see p54)* and the Sulabh International Museum of Toilets *(see p55)*.

4 Open-Air Gyms

Those looking for a free outdoor workout are in luck. The New Delhi Municipal Council has installed an array of fitness equipment in the Lodi Gardens *(see pp30–31)* and Nehru Park *(see p59)*, and now plans to roll them out in parks across the city.

5 Changing of the Guard

MAP L3 ▪ Gate No. 2 Rashtrapati Bhavan, Rajpath ▪ Sat & Sun, check website for timings ▪ www.rb.nic.in/rbvisit/visit_plan.aspx

Although visits to see the interior of the presidential palace *(see pp20–21)* incur a small booking fee, the weekly Changing of the Guard ceremony is free; just bring your passport.

The Changing of the Guard

6 Hindu temples

All Hindu temples are free to enter as long as you dress respectfully. The most popular are three modern temples – Lakshmi Narayan Mandir *(see p79)*, Akshardham Temple *(see p94)* and Chhattarpur Mandir *(see p61)* – and the Gauri Shankar Mandir in Old Delhi *(see p88)*.

7 Hauz Khas
MAP U2 ■ Hauz Khas Village Road

Alauddin Khilji's 14th-century Hauz-i-Alai reservoir *(see p100)* is free to visit, as is the nearby Deer Park *(see p58)*. The road into the village from Aurobindo Marg has a string of 14th- and 15th-century tombs along it; these are also free to everyone.

8 Jahanpanah
MAP W2 ■ Between the Outer Ring Road, Press Enclave Marg, Aurobindo Marg and Lal Bahadur Shastri Marg

Delhi's fourth incarnation *(see p51)* is full of fascinating free sights, from the Begumpuri Masjid *(see p100)* and Bijay Mandal *(see p61)* to the Khirki Masjid *(see p45)* and Chiragh Delhi village *(p101)*. Combined, they add up to a wonderful half-day walk.

9 Qawwalis in Nizamuddin

Anyone can attend the *dargah* at Nizamuddin *(see p94)* to hear *qawwalis*, the rhythmic chanting and singing used by devotees to achieve a trance-like state. Visitors should dress respectfully, as this is a religious shrine. It is also home to a cluster of Mughal monuments and the graves of various notable individuals, including poet and musician Amir Khusrau (1253–1325), Shah Jahan's daughter Jahanara and the great Urdu poet Mirza Ghalib *(see p88)*.

10 Gurudwara Bangla Sahib

Delhi's biggest Sikh temple *(see p52)* offers free guided tours on request, with devotional music on tap, and a free meal of *dal* and *chapattis* three times daily for everyone.

TOP 10 BUDGET TIPS

Auto-rickshaws in Old Delhi

1 For auto-rickshaws, use the pre paid booths at Connaught Place, Janpath and transport terminals, paying an official set rate to avoid overcharging.

2 The metro is much cheaper than a taxi or auto-rickshaw, and usually faster, with no haggling.

3 You don't need to buy your holiday reading before your trip: bookshops in Delhi stock the latest bestsellers. There are also a number of second-hand booksellers *(see p67)* in the city.

4 Most bars in Delhi have a happy hour early in the evening, typically with "buy one get one free" offers on Indian beers and spirits.

5 A coffee at the India Coffee House *(see p82)* costs about a quarter of the price charged by other high-end espresso chains.

6 Alternatively, drink tea: a nice, warming cup of *pukka chai* will cost around ten rupees on any street corner.

7 Have a meal at a *dhaba* (local diner). If the food is freshly cooked, then hygiene shouldn't be an issue. If the menu isn't in English, it's a good idea to confirm the price before ordering.

8 A couple of Delhi's best restaurants offer slightly less expensive set menus. At Bukhara *(see p65)*, there's a lunch-time set menu, while Spice Route *(see p64)*, by contrast, has a tasting menu in the evening.

9 It is possible to get a bespoke suit made by a tailor at Connaught Place, such as M Ram and Sons *(see p81)*.

10 A ticket for the Taj Mahal gives travellers a discounted rate for entry to Fatehpur Sikri and several sites around Agra if they go on the same day.

TOP 10 Festivals and Events

A marching regiment at the Indian Republic Day Parade

1 Republic Day Parade
26 Jan

India's biggest parade celebrates the inauguration of the Indian constitution on 26 January 1950. The parade begins at the foot of Raisina Hill *(see p20)* and ends at the Red Fort, with military march pasts, floats and a fly-past by the Indian Air Force.

2 Beating the Retreat
29 Jan

Signalling the official end of the Republic Day celebrations, this ceremony recalls the old battlefield tradition of soldiers halting hostilities at the end of the day. It is held at Vijay Chowk *(see p21)* and features a parade of soldiers accompanied by military bands.

3 Surajkund Crafts Mela
A fortnight in Feb

Held in Surajkund, about 20 km (12 miles) south of Delhi, this is one of India's biggest craft fairs, showcasing works from all over the country, with musicians and dancers creating a lively carnivalesque atmosphere.

Surajkund Crafts Mela handicrafts

4 Vintage Car Rally
Late Feb/Early Mar

This car rally features around 100 vintage and postwar cars, with their owners dressed in period costume. The event starts and ends in central Delhi and attracts participants from all over the country.

5 National School of Drama Festivals
May and Jun ■ Adm

Each year, the National School of Drama *(see p62)* hosts the Summer Theatre Festival, with a variety of classical and contemporary plays staged by the school's professional repertory company. In spring, it hosts the Bharat Rang Mahotsav, with plays by theatre companies from across the world.

6 International Mango Festival
Late Jun/Early Jul

Mango lovers can sample more than 500 different types of mango that are on offer at this annual celebration of the delicious yellow fruit. The event is held at held at Talkatora Gardens *(see p58)* every year.

7 Phool Walon ki Sair
Usually 3 days in Sep

The colourful Festival of the Flower Sellers is held in Mehrauli (see p100) after the rainy season. The highlight is the procession of flower sellers, who carry ornate floral tributes to the shrine of Qutb Sahib (see p26). They are led by dancers and people playing the *shehnai*, a type of woodwind instrument whose sound is thought to create a sense of sanctity.

8 The IIC Experience
Mid-Oct

Held at the IIC (see p63), this festival of the arts hosts a wide range of cultural events from music and dance (both Indian and Western) to theatre, film and literature, and is accompanied by a good food festival.

9 Qutb Festival
Nov/Dec

A three-day music festival, with concerts held in the Qutb Minar Complex (see pp24–5), ranging from soulful *qawwali* singers and virtuoso sitar players to young rock bands.

A cosplayer at Delhi Comic Con

10 Delhi Comic Con
Dec

Held over three days, this pop culture fest showcases the works of Indian and international comic artists. Similar to other comic cons held around the world, the Delhi edition also features comedy performances, panel discussions, and entertaining cosplay competitions.

TOP 10 RELIGIOUS FESTIVALS

A devotee with an idol of Ganesh

1 Maha Shivaratri
Late Feb/early Mar
The "Great Night of Shiva" is marked with fasts and prayers.

2 Holi
Mar
Hindu spring festival where people douse each other with colour and water.

3 Rama Navami
Late Mar/early Apr
Celebration of the birth of Rama, with continuous readings of the *Ramayana*.

4 Buddha Jayanti
May
Festival celebrating the Buddha's birth, enlightenment and death.

5 Krishna Janmashtami
Mid-Aug–mid-Sep
Celebration of the birth of Lord Krishna.

6 Ganesh Chaturthi
Mid-Aug–mid-Sep
Ten-day festival celebrating the birth of Lord Ganesh with colourful processions.

7 Dussehra
Mid-Sep–mid-Oct
Ten-day celebration of the victory of good over evil, including Rama's over Ravana and Durga's over Mahishasura.

8 Bakr Id
Sep/Oct
The year's biggest Muslim festival, when the Jama Masjid area becomes a market for sacrificial goats.

9 Diwali
Oct/Nov
Five-day festival of lights honouring Rama's return to Ayodhya from exile.

10 Guru Purab
All year
Ten Sikh festivals, each celebrating the birth of one of the Sikh faith's ten gurus.

TOP **10** Excursions from Delhi

A monkey outside Mathura temple

3 Deeg
MAP B3 ■ Deeg Palace: open 8am–5pm daily ■ Adm

This workaday town is home to one of the region's most spectacular palaces. Built in the 18th century by the local Jat rulers, the Deeg Palace blends Hindu and Mughal elements with spacious water gardens dotted with palaces and pavilions. The celebrated Keshav Bhawan (known as Monsoon Palace) was designed to re-create the torrential rainfall and thunderous sounds of a wet-season downpour.

1 Mathura and Vrindavan
MAP C3

Mathura is reputed to be the birth place of the flute-playing deity, Krishna, while half a million pilgrims a year flock to the nearby town of Vrindavan and the hill of Govardhan, which Krishna is said to have lifted with just a single finger.

2 Amritsar
MAP B1

The holiest city of the Sikh faith is home to the Golden Temple, an unforgettable sight with the gilded Harmandir Sahib rising out of the surrounding lake.

4 Sultanpur Bird Sanctuary
MAP B3 ■ 45 km (28 miles) SW of Delhi ■ Open 6am–4:30pm Wed–Mon ■ Adm and charge for video

Kingfisher in Sultanpur Bird Sanctuary

About 45 km (28 miles) southwest of Delhi in Haryana state, the Sultanpur Bird Sanctuary makes for a peaceful rural outing. Centred on a large wetland area that fills up during the seasonal rains, the sanctuary attracts aquatic migratory birds and offers a number of walks through the surrounding woods.

5 Keoladeo Ghana National Park
MAP C3 ■ Bharatpur district, 185 km (115 miles) E of Jaipur ■ Open Apr–Sep: 6am–6pm; Oct–Mar: 6:30am–5:30pm ■ Adm

This wonderful national park near the town of Bharatpur is arguably India's finest birdwatching destination. It is home to a huge number of resident and migratory species, including flocks of aquatic birds who come to nest in the park's wetlands.

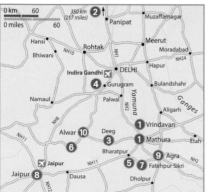

6 Sariska Tiger Reserve

MAP B3 ■ Alwar district, 37 km (23 miles) SW of Alwar ■ Alwar tourist office: 0144 234 7348 ■ Open 6am–4pm daily (call in advance to check for timings)

An hour's drive beyond Alwar, the Sariska Tiger Reserve was left without any tigers in 2005, when it was discovered that the park's entire tiger population had vanished, presumably taken by poachers. With a re-population programme, the number of tigers is now believed to be 14. The visitors can also see a wide range of birdlife and a good selection of Indian mammals, ranging from jackals to antelopes.

7 Fatehpur Sikri

MAP C3 ■ Open sunrise–sunset daily ■ Adm

Around 40 km (25 miles) beyond Agra lie the fascinating remains of the ghost city of Fatehpur Sikri, built by Akbar between 1569 and 1585, but abandoned not long afterwards. The city remains wonderfully preserved, with superb red sandstone buildings and a magically time-warped atmosphere.

8 Jaipur

MAP B3

Jaipur, the capital of Rajasthan, is a fascinating city with many attractions, ranging from the bazaars of the old Pink City to the City Palace and the Hawa Mahal, whose five-storey façade is one of India's most famous sights.

9 Agra

Once capital of the entire Mughal Empire, the large and chaotic city of Agra is home to some of India's most wonderful and inspiring monuments, including the impressive Agra Fort, the exquisite Itimad-ud-Daulah, Emperor Akbar's Tomb at Sikandra and, of course, the magnificent Taj Mahal *(see pp36–9)*.

The city of Alwar in Rajasthan

10 Alwar

MAP B3

Midway between Delhi and Jaipur, the characterful little city of Alwar is considered the traditional northern gateway to Rajasthan. It boasts an imposing fort with ramparts cresting a series of hills above the town, and an absorbing old city palace below.

Ornate design of Jaipur's Hawa Mahal

Delhi Area by Area

Humayun's Tomb, a stunning
example of Mughal architecture

 New Delhi

The city of New Delhi, built by the British between 1911 and 1931, still serves as the hub of Delhi's increasingly huge and formless urban expanse. The area is divided into two parts. The first is Connaught Place – a huge, vibrant circular plaza of Georgian crescents, that is home to shops, restaurants and other businesses, and is located at the commercial and residential heart of the city. The second, some 2 km (1 mile) south down Janpath, is the great Imperial thoroughfare of Rajpath, linking a triumphalist sequence of Raj-era landmarks, including India Gate and the Rashtrapati Bhavan. The area is also home to almost all the city's finest museums, plus a few relics dating back to the years before British rule.

Sunga Dynasty sculpture, National Museum

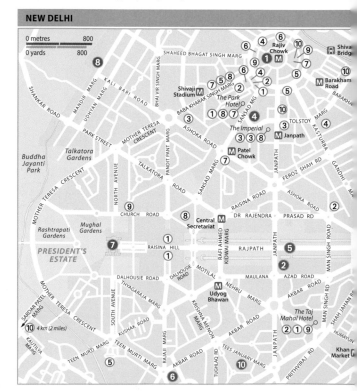

NEW DELHI

Neo-Classical buildings at Connaught Place

plaza occupies a pivotal position in the layout of the new city, with roads radiating off in every direction. Built around a central park, it is surrounded by colonnaded white Neo-Classical buildings, their shaded arcades hosting shops and restaurants.

1 Connaught Place (CP)
MAP F6 ■ Rajiv Chowk Metro

The commercial hub of New Delhi, Connaught Place, or CP (now officially rechristened Rajiv Chowk), was built between 1929 and 1933 to a design by British architect Robert Tor Russell. The enormous circular

---

1 Top 10 Sights
see pp77–9

1 Places to Eat
see p83

1 Places to Shop
see p81

1 The Best of the Rest
see p80

1 Bars and Cafés
see p82

---

2 National Museum

This is India's largest and most impressive museum (see pp32–5) with a vast collection of artifacts from prehistory to the 20th century. Highlights include a superb selection of ancient finds from the Harappan Civilization and an excellent collection of Indian miniatures, alongside Hindu and Buddhist sculpture. Also on display is an array of wonderful Chola bronzes including a famous statuette of the dancing Shiva.

3 India Gate

At the eastern end of Rajpath (see p20) stands India Gate, built in 1931 to a design by architect Edwin Lutyens, who also designed the Cenotaph on London's Whitehall. The monument was originally known as the All India War Memorial, built to commemorate the 90,000 soldiers of the British Indian Army killed during World War I and the Afghan Wars. The Tomb of the Unknown Soldier, or Amar Jawan Jyoti, was added in 1971.

Historic India Gate

Observatory at the Jantar Mantar

4 Jantar Mantar
MAP F7 ▪ Sansad Marg ▪ Janpath Metro ▪ Open sunrise–sunset daily ▪ www.jantarmantar.org ▪ Adm

The Jantar Mantar was one of five outdoor astronomical observatories constructed by the Maharaja of Jaipur, Jai Singh II (the others are in Jaipur, Mathura, Varanasi and Ujjain). Built in 1724, it consists of four huge, strangely shaped stone instruments; these include the Samrat Yantra, a kind of monumental sundial centred on an enormous stone staircase, and the Misra Yantra, shaped like a huge inverted heart. The instruments were designed to perform various functions, including measuring exact solar and lunar calendars and tracking the movements of stars and accurate planetary positions.

5 Rajpath
Originally named Kingsway, Rajpath *(see pp20–21)* is the ceremonial axis of Lutyens' New Delhi and links most of the major landmarks of the "new city". It runs all the way from India Gate via Vijay Chowk up Raisina Hill, between the two Secretariat Buildings and on to Rashtrapati Bhavan. The main section, between India Gate and Vijay Chowk, forms Delhi's most impressive open space: a huge sprawling boulevard flanked by lawns, with dramatic views of the Imperial monuments in every direction.

6 Indira Gandhi Memorial Museum
MAP M5 ▪ 1 Safdarjung Road ▪ 2301 0094 ▪ Open 9:30am–5pm Tue–Sun

Formerly home to both Indira Gandhi and her son, Rajiv, this moving museum is also the site of Indira's assassination (1984) by two of her Sikh bodyguards. There is a wide-ranging array of displays on Indira's years in power, offering a glimpse into both her achievements and lapses into quasi-dictatorship, as well as an extensive collection of Rajiv's personal effects.

CURSE OF THE CITY BUILDERS

An old Persian prophecy claims that "Whoever builds a new city in Delhi will lose it". Several rulers of the city have experienced the force of this curse, but the most spectacular fall from grace was that of the British, who spent around 20 years building New Delhi, only to be forced out within 14 years of the city's completion.

7 Rashtrapati Bhavan
The centrepiece of New Delhi and generally regarded as Lutyens' masterpiece, the Rashtrapati Bhavan *(see p21)* is the residence of the President of India. It is India's finest example of Colonial-era architecture. The work is a remarkable synthesis of Neo-Classical and Indian styles, exemplified by the huge dome, said to have been modelled partly on the Pantheon in Rome and partly on the Buddhist stupa at Sanchi.

Exterior of Rashtrapati Bhavan

8 Lakshmi Narayan Mandir

MAP D6 ■ Mandir Marg, near Connaught Place ■ R K Ashram Marg Metro ■ Open 4:30am–noon & 2–9pm daily ■ No cameras or mobile phones allowed

Built in 1938 by industrialist BD Birla, this temple is the biggest and most striking of the various shrines along Mandir Marg, with a clustered mass of red-and-orange *shikharas* (towers) centred on a large marble courtyard. Shrines to Durga and a meditating statue of Shiva stand within.

Lakshmi Narayan Mandir

9 Crafts Museum

One of Delhi's most engaging and entertaining sights, the Crafts Museum (see pp28–9) offers an alternative take on the nation's cultural heritage. In contrast to the classic artworks at the National Museum, the emphasis here is on local artisanal traditions, showcasing an incredibly varied – and often quirky – range of cultural, religious and architectural traditions from all over the subcontinent.

10 Gandhi Smriti

MAP N5 ■ 5 Tees January Marg ■ 2301 2843 ■ Open 10am–5pm Tue–Sun

It was here in 1948 that a Hindu fundamentalist assassinated Gandhi. The museum simultaneously serves as an absorbing exposition of Gandhi's life and work and also as a shrine to one of the 20th-century's most inspirational leaders. Stone footsteps mark the route of Gandhi's last walk.

A DAY IN NEW DELHI

▶ MORNING

Begin your day exploring the varied exhibits at the engaging **Crafts Museum** (see pp28–9), then walk along to the eastern end of **Rajpath** and **India Gate** (see p77). Continue on to the **National Museum** (see p77) to spend a couple more hours browsing its superb range of Indian artifacts. Stop for a snack at the museum's small café, or alternatively take an auto-rickshaw down to **Khan Market** (see p67), which has a wide variety of restaurants and cafés from which to choose. Have lunch at SodaBottleOpenerWala (see p97) or Latitude 28 Café (see p97).

AFTERNOON

Continue walking west along the stately expanse of **Rajpath**, as Herbert Baker's Neo-Classical **Secretariat Buildings** (see p80) come gradually into view. Carry on to the top of Raisina Hill for a peek at Lutyens' masterpiece, **Rashtrapati Bhavan**; visits can be arranged by calling in advance (see p21). From here, catch an auto-rickshaw, or walk north via **Sansad Bhavan** (see p80), to the 18th-century outdoor astronomical park of **Jantar Mantar**. Take your time inspecting the intriguing planetary instruments here, then walk 100 metres (110 yards) north to **Connaught Place** (see p77), the heart of commercial New Delhi. Finish the day with a snack at one of the area's many restaurants (see p83), or a drink at the bars and cafés (see p82).

See map on pp76–7 ←

The Best of the Rest

1 Secretariat Buildings

MAP M3 ■ Raisina Hill

Herbert Baker's grandiose Secretariat Buildings, framing Raisina Hill, are two of the city's finest examples of epic Neo-Classical style.

Crest, Secretariat Buildings

2 Hanuman Mandir

MAP F7 ■ Baba Kharak Singh Marg ■ timings vary; check website ■ www.hanumantempledelhi.com

This temple boasts a richly decorated interior, full of religious atmosphere.

3 Gurudwara Bangla Sahib

MAP E7 ■ Ashoka Road ■ Open daily ■ www.banglasahib.org

The Bangla Sahib is Delhi's most important Sikh *gurudwara* (temple).

4 Agrasen's Baoli

MAP G7 ■ Off Hailey Road, Kasturba Gandhi Marg ■ Open daily

This spectacularly deep *baoli* (stepwell), now dry, is thought to have been built by Raja Agrasen (or Ugrasen) in the 14th century.

Agrasen's impressive *baoli*

5 Jawaharlal Nehru Memorial Museum

MAP L5 ■ Teen Murti Marg ■ 2301 7587 ■ Open 9am–5:30pm Tue–Sun

The former home of India's first prime minister, with a series of period interiors preserved exactly as they were in Nehru's time.

6 National Gallery of Modern Art (NGMA)

MAP Q3 ■ Jaipur House ■ 2338 6111 ■ Open 10am–6pm Tue–Sun ■ www.ngmaindia.gov.in

This gallery has an outstanding range of Colonial and modern Indian art.

7 National Philatelic Museum

MAP N2 ■ Dak Bhawan, Sardar Patel Chowk, Sansad Marg ■ 2303 6447 ■ Open 10am–5pm Mon–Fri

A philatelic paradise, with displays covering every stamp issued by India since independence, as well as some older, but well-preserved, exhibits.

8 Sansad Bhavan

MAP M2 ■ Lok Sabha Marg ■ Closed to the public

Designed by Lutyens, this edifice is home to the Indian parliament.

9 Cathedral Church of the Redemption

MAP L2 ■ 1 Church Road, North Avenue ■ Open 9am–6pm daily

This is Delhi's grandest Anglican church and one of the city's last major Raj-era buildings (1931).

10 St Martin's Church

MAP A6 ■ Off Cariappa Marg, near Dhaula Kuan and NH8

Built in 1930, this was one of Britain's architectural ventures. It is one of Delhi's most unusual churches.

Places to Shop

1 The Shop
MAP F6 ■ 10 Regal Building, Connaught Place ■ 2334 0971 ■ Open 9:30am–7:30pm Mon–Sat, noon–7pm Sun

The Shop is excellent for ethnic Indian homewares and lifestyle products.

The Shop, ideal for gifts

2 People Tree
MAP F6 ■ 8 Regal Building, Parliament Road, Connaught Place ■ 2374 4877 ■ Open 10am–8pm Mon–Sat

The imaginative and colourful apparel here is created by socially and environmentally conscious artists and designers.

3 Central Cottage Industries Emporium
MAP F7 ■ Jawahar Vyapar Bhavan, Janpath ■ 2332 0439 ■ Open 10am–7pm daily

This government initiative was set up to preserve and develop handicrafts from all over the country.

4 Khadi
MAP F6 ■ Khadi Gramodyog Bhavan, 24 Regal Building, Connaught Place ■ 2336 0902 ■ Open 11am–7pm daily

A government initiative, Khadi supports the production of Indian fabrics, natural cosmetics, organic food, pottery and handmade paper.

5 Tribes India
MAP F7 ■ Gallery 2, Rajiv Gandhi Handicrafts Bhavan, Baba Kharak Singh Marg ■ 2334 1282 ■ Open 10am–9pm Mon–Sat

A store that stocks some lovely tribal handicrafts from all over the country.

6 Soma
MAP F6 ■ K-44 Connaught Place ■ 2341 2966 ■ Open 10am–8pm daily

Wonderful dresses, fabrics and home furnishings, block-printed by hand using a traditional Indian method.

7 Kamala
MAP F7 ■ Gallery 1, Rajiv Gandhi Handicrafts Bhavan, Baba Kharak Singh Marg ■ 2374 3321 ■ Open 10am–7pm Mon–Sat

Kamala offers exotic jewellery, folk paintings, pottery, bric-a-brac and handwoven and printed fabrics.

8 State Emporia Complex
MAP F6 ■ Pallika Kendra, Baba Kharak Singh Marg ■ Shivaji Stadium Metro ■ Open 11am–6:30pm Mon–Sat

Visitors can explore and shop from an array of regional merchandise, from paintings to crafts, from saris to jewellery, and much more.

9 Rikhi Ram
MAP F6 ■ G-8 Connaught Place ■ 2332 7685 ■ Open 11am–8pm Mon–Sat

Many musicians, such as the late Ravi Shankar, have bought their sitars and tablas from this long-established firm, still crafting traditional musical instruments the old-fashioned way.

10 M Ram and Sons
MAP F6 ■ E-21 Connaught Place ■ 2341 6558 ■ Open 10am–8pm Mon–Sat (Sep–Feb: 11am–7pm Sun)

This excellent tailoring firm, in business since 1939, can make up a bespoke suit in no time at all, for a fraction of department store prices.

See map on pp76

Bars and Cafés

The glamorous outdoor space, overlooking the pool, at Aqua

1 Aqua
MAP F7 ▪ The Park, 15 Parliament Street ▪ 2374 3000 ▪ Open 11am–midnight daily

A glamorous alfresco bar and dining space complete with a pool and chic white-curtained pavilions.

2 Rick's
MAP P4 ▪ The Taj Mahal Hotel, 1 Man Singh Road ▪ 2302 6162 ▪ Open 4pm–1am daily

Everyone's favourite in town, Rick's *(see p65)* is an understated and intimate bar with an extensive wine list.

3 1911
MAP F7 ▪ The Imperial, 1 Janpath ▪ 4111 6604 ▪ Open 11:30–12:45am daily

Replete with old-world charm, 1911 is best enjoyed on a sunny afternoon over a chilled beer.

4 Triveni Tea Terrace
MAP Q1 ▪ Triveni Kala Sangam, 205 Tansen Marg ▪ 99715 66904 ▪ Open 10am–9pm Mon–Sat, noon–9pm Sun

Sharing space with four art galleries, this is a charming spot for relaxing.

5 Cha Bar
MAP G7 ▪ N-81 Barakhamba Road, Connaught Place ▪ 99580 05985 ▪ Open 9:30am–9:30pm Mon–Sat

Housed in the Oxford Bookstore, the Cha Bar offers an extensive tea list.

6 India Coffee House (ICH)
MAP F7 ▪ 2nd floor, Mohan Singh Place Shopping Complex, Baba Kharak Singh Marg, off Connaught Place ▪ 2334 2994 ▪ Open 9am–9pm daily

The venerable ICH serves excellent south Indian coffee at low prices.

7 Q'BA
MAP F6 ▪ E-42/43 Connaught Place ▪ 4517 3333 ▪ Open noon–1am daily

The terrace has fairy lights and a great view of Connaught Place.

8 Agni
MAP F7 ▪ The Park, 15 Parliament Street ▪ 2374 3000 ▪ Open 5pm–12:30am, days vary, call ahead

Loud and fun, Agni is a great place for *bhangra* (Punjabi dance).

9 Ministry of Beer
MAP G6 ▪ M-44, Outer Circle, Connaught Place ▪ 88001 19277 ▪ Open noon–12:30am daily

A great place to unwind, this bar has a wide selection of beer and quirky cocktails on offer.

10 Kitty Su
MAP G6 ▪ Lalit Hotel, Tolstoy Marg, off Barakhamba Road ▪ 4444 7666 ▪ Open 10pm–1am Wed–Sun

There is mainly electronic music at this vibrant hotel nightclub with DJs, regular concerts and parties.

Places to Eat

1 Wasabi by Morimoto

MAP P4 ■ The Taj Mahal Hotel, 1 Man Singh Road ■ 2302 6162 ■ Open 12:30–2:45pm & 7–11:30pm daily ■ ₹₹₹

This swanky restaurant *(see p65)* serves excellent Japanese food.

2 Andhra Bhawan

MAP P2 ■ 1 Ashoka Road ■ 2338 2031 ■ Open 8–10:30am, noon–3:30pm & 7:30–10pm daily ■ ₹

The finest spicy Andhra food, served at extremely reasonable prices.

3 Spice Route

MAP F7 ■ The Imperial, 1 Janpath ■ 2334 1234 ■ Open 12:30–2:30pm & 7–11:30pm daily ■ ₹₹₹

Fine cuisine inspired by places along the Spice Route *(see p64)*.

4 Veda

MAP F6 ■ H-27 Connaught Place ■ 4151 3535 ■ Open noon–11:30pm daily ■ ₹₹

An opulent restaurant that serves top-notch food – from the *murgh malai tikka* to Parsi sea bass.

5 Rajdhani

MAP F6 ■ 9-A Atmaram Mansion, Scindia House, Connaught Place ■ 4350 1200 ■ Open noon–3:30pm & 7–11pm daily ■ ₹

Serving up almost-authentic Gujarati food, this no-frills place is great for a vegetarian thali.

6 Bombay Brasserie

MAP F6 ■ H-66-68, Connaught Place ■ 4003 0500 ■ Open 11am–midnight daily ■ ₹₹

This trendy restaurant is popular for its modern take on classic Indian dishes.

7 Fire

MAP F7 ■ The Park, 15 Parliament Street ■ 2374 3000 ■ Open 12:30–2:45pm & 7:30–11:45pm daily ■ ₹₹₹

A smart, contemporary restaurant serving fine modern Indian cuisine, with a seasonal menu, light in summer, fiery hot in winter.

8 Daniell's Tavern

MAP F7 ■ The Imperial, 1 Janpath ■ 2334 1234 ■ Open 6:30–11:45pm daily ■ ₹₹₹

This is a lovely, elegant place, inspired by the travels of the late 18th-century artists Thomas and William Daniell, and serving up plates of first-rate Indian cuisine.

9 Varq

MAP P4 ■ The Taj Mahal Hotel, 1 Man Singh Road ■ 2302 6162 ■ Open 12:30–2:45pm & 7–11:30pm daily ■ ₹₹₹

A stylish, relaxed restaurant, Varq serves truly delicious Indian food. Try the lamb cooked in a saffron crust or the excellent crispy Calicut prawns.

Dining space at stylish restaurant Varq

10 Saravana Bhavan

MAP F7 ■ 50 Janpath ■ 2331 7755 ■ Open 8am–11pm daily ■ ₹

When it comes to authentic South Indian food in Delhi, Saravana Bhavan *(see p64)* is the place to go. The mini-tiffin is great.

See map on pp76–7

TOP 10 Old Delhi

The city of Shahjahanabad was originally built by Mughal emperor Shah Jahan between 1638 to 1648 to replace the previous Mughal capital of Agra. Now generally known as Old Delhi, is the most rewarding part of the city. This is Delhi at its most traditional and atmospheric: a fascinating labyrinth of tiny alleyways, colourful bazaars and a profusion of historical monuments and religious shrines, including two of Delhi's landmark attractions: the magnificent Red Fort and the grand Jama Masjid. There are further – albeit more modest – points of interest north of Old Delhi in the quiet Civil Lines district, where the British first established themselves in the city, and along the lush Northern Ridge, where they sought refuge during the opening months of the 1857 Uprising.

Shakti Sthal, Raj Ghat

OLD DELHI

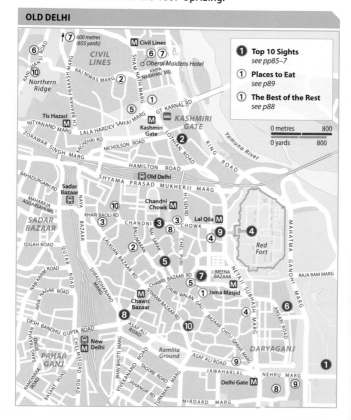

1 **Top 10 Sights**
see pp85–7

1 **Places to Eat**
see p89

1 **The Best of the Rest**
see p88

1 Raj Ghat
MAP J5 ■ Mahatma Gandhi Marg ■ Open sunrise–sunset daily

These spacious gardens, set back from the banks of the Yamuna River, are best known as the place where the funeral rites of many of modern India's most important leaders were performed. Most notable among these is perhaps Gandhi, who was cremated here in 1948, and whose simple marble memorial still draws large crowds of reverent visitors. Other memorials dot the lawns, marking the places of the funeral sites of other national leaders, including Shanti Vana (Jawaharlal Nehru), Shakti Sthal (Indira Gandhi) and Vir Bhumi (Rajiv Gandhi).

2 St James' Church
MAP G2 ■ Sham Nath Marg ■ Kashmiri Gate Metro ■ Open 9am–1pm & 2–5pm daily

This little Neo-Classical gem was built by Colonel James Skinner in 1836 – a perfect period piece, constructed in an unusual cruciform pattern with a large dome over the central crossing. In and around the church stand memorials to some of the city's most colourful early British residents, including William Fraser, Thomas Metcalfe (see p27) and Colonel James Skinner himself.

3 Chandni Chowk
Old Delhi's main thoroughfare, and one of the most colourful streets in Delhi, Chandni Chowk (see pp14–15)

A market stall at Chandni Chowk

runs dead straight from the gates of the Red Fort due west to the Fatehpuri Masjid (see p15), passing a range of shops and shrines en route. The road's name, meaning Moonlit Square, is said to refer to a square that once stood about halfway along the road, and which was known for the moonlit reflections in the canal that ran through its centre.

4 Red Fort
The enormous Red Fort (see pp12–13) served as the residence of the Mughal emperors from its completion in 1648 through to the 1857 Uprising, when the last emperor, Bahadur Shah Zafar II, was exiled to Burma and the British took over the fort, demolishing many of its buildings. What is left now is only a shadow of the original complex, but the surviving pavilions and gardens still give a sense of the sophisticated lifestyles of India's most powerful and cultured rulers.

The impressive Red Fort

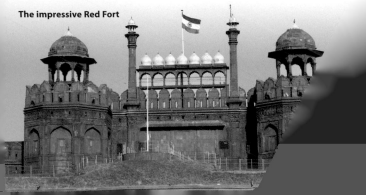

5 Bazaars of Old Delhi

Although much of the physical fabric of Old Delhi is fairly modern – due to damage sustained during the 1857 Uprising and 20th-century rebuilding – the entire area retains its original, labyrinthine street plan and much of its traditional atmosphere. Different areas have bazaars (see pp66–7) devoted to different trades and crafts – from jewellery and wedding gifts to fireworks and even some spare car parts.

Colourful Kinari bazaar in Old Delhi

6 Zinat ul Masjid

MAP J4 ■ Ghata Masjid Road, Daryaganj ■ Taxi or rickshaw ■ Open sunrise–sunset daily

Hidden away in the streets of Daryaganj, this lovely mosque was commissioned in 1707 by Zinat ul Nisa, Aurangzeb's daughter, and is popularly known as the Ghata Masjid. Zinat ul Nisa was buried here in 1711, but her tomb was apparently removed by the British after the Uprising, when the mosque was taken over for military use.

7 Jama Masjid

The Jama Masjid (see pp16–17) is unquestionably the most beautiful of Old Delhi's Mughal monuments, looming high above the surrounding streets on a natural hillock and dominating all views of the old city. The approach from Meena Bazaar up to the eastern gate, facing the Red Fort, is particularly dramatic, although visitors now have to enter via the rather less imposing gateway on the western side.

8 Ajmeri Gate

MAP G4 ■ Ajmeri Gate Road ■ Chawri Bazaar Metro

Marooned on a small island amidst busy traffic, this is perhaps the most impressive of the four surviving gateways that once punctuated the old city walls. The fine old *madrasa* and Mosque of Ghazi-ud-Din, built in classic Mughal style, stand just opposite. Elsewhere in the old city, the Delhi, Kashmiri and Turkman gates also survive in good condition – the last is named after the revered Sufi saint, Hazrat Shah Turkman.

…mes and arches at the Zinat ul Masjid mosque

The rounded Lal Mandir temple

9 Lal Mandir

Delhi's most important Jain temple, Lal Mandir (see p14) is located directly opposite the Red Fort, at the southern end of Chandni Chowk. Founded under Shah Jahan for the Jain soldiers in his army, the present building dates from the 1870s. The colourful interior is adorned with dozens of diminutive statues of various Jain tirthankaras. The temple's well-known bird hospital stands next door, caring for hundreds of hungry and injured pigeons and other birds, in tiny cages.

HAZRAT SHAH TURKMAN

Delhi's Turkman Gate is named after a *bayabani* ("jungle dwelling") Sufi hermit, Hazrat Shah Turkman (d. 1240), who lived nearby when the area was still forest. Despite his seclusion, his fame as a holy man spread, and many sought him out. His tiny *dargah* (tomb and mosque) is hidden away in the back alleys. Razia Sultan, a devoted follower of his, was buried nearby.

10 Tomb of Razia Sultan

MAP G4 ▪ Off Sitaram Bazaar Road ▪ Chawri Bazaar Metro ▪ Open sunrise–sunset daily

The tomb is in a roofless enclosure that was built here long before the city that surrounds it for its proximity to Turkman's tomb. The only female monarch until Queen Victoria to rule a vast swathe of the subcontinent, Razia was loved by the people but hated by the aristocracy, who resented having a woman as their ruler and overthrew her after a four-year reign.

A DAY IN OLD DELHI

 MORNING

Start your day at the Red Fort (see p85) – arrive early to avoid the crowds. Spend a couple of hours exploring the complex; stop at the food stall outside the main gate for a quick bite. Exit the fort and walk up Chandni Chowk (see p85), stopping by the various attractions en route. Stop at Haldiram's (see p89), halfway up the road, for a tasty Indian fast-food lunch, then cross the road to Kanwarji's, established in 1850 and Delhi's oldest sweet shop since the closure of the famed Ghantewala's, founded in 1790 and once purveyor of sweets to the Mughal emperors.

AFTERNOON

Carry on up Chandni Chowk to the Fatehpuri Masjid (see p15), then on to the remarkable spice market of Khari Baoli (see p66), just beyond. From here, you can either retrace your steps down Chandni Chowk, then turn right down Dariba Kalan, or alternatively head down Ballimaran (see p66) to visit the *haveli* of the great Urdu poet Mirza Ghalib (see p88) and then Chawri Bazaar, through the heart of Old Delhi's bazaar. Much of the fun lies in simply wandering at will; aim to s... at least once. Whichever ... you take, be at the Ja... towards sunset, wh... mosque is at its r... able, and the vi... city and Red F... best. On lea... you will b... of Karim... Delhi'... a p...

The Best of the Rest

1 Qudsia Bagh
MAP G1 ■ Lala Hardev Sahai Marg ■ Open sunrise–sunset daily
These are lovely, peaceful wooded gardens, just north of the old city, and home to a couple of very fine buildings dating back to the gardens' foundation during the 18th century.

Qudsia Bagh

2 Mirza Ghalib Haveli
MAP G3 ■ Qasimjan Street, off Ballimaran ■ Open 10am–5pm Tue–Sun
The former home of the great Urdu poet Mirza Ghalib (1797–1869) has been carefully restored and is now a simple museum, with a few exhibits on the writer's life and times.

3 Hauzwali Mosque
MAP G5 ■ Chandni Chowk ■ Chandni Chowk Metro ■ Open sunrise–sunset daily
This little blue mosque is one of the few surviving buildings from the time of Suri ruler Sher Khan.

4 Gauri Shankar Mandir
MAP H3 ■ Chandni Chowk
Old Delhi's largest and ~lar Hindu temples, ~ar Mandir (see p15) ~ Shiva (Shankar) ~ri).

has the grave of Brigadier-General John Nicholson, who led the British assault on Delhi in 1857.

6 Pir Ghaib
MAP F1 ■ Ridge Road ■ Open daily
Rising up north of Old Delhi is the long, forested Northern Ridge, dotted with British and Tughlaq monuments, such as the ruins of Pir Ghaib, a hunting lodge built by Feroz Shah Tughlaq in the 14th century.

7 Chauburji Masjid
MAP B4 ■ Magazine Road ■ Open sunrise–sunset daily
A Tughlaq-era ruins in the Northern Ridge, this structure was built as a tomb around 1345, and subsequently converted into a mosque.

8 Feroz Shah Kotla
MAP J6 ■ Bahadur Shah Zafar Marg ■ Open sunrise–sunset daily
All that remains of Sultan Feroz Shah Tughlaq's erstwhile citadel – now popularly thought to be the abode of djinns (spirits).

9 National Gandhi Museum
MAP J5 ■ Jawaharlal Nehru Marg, opposite Raj Ghat ■ 2331 0168 ■ Open 9:30am–5:30pm Tue–Sun (closed Mon & public hols) ■ www.gandhimuseum.org
At the southern end of the expansive Raj Ghat gardens, this engaging little museum offers some endearingly personal insights into the Mahatma's remarkable life and works.

10 Ashoka Column
MAP E1 ■ Rani Jhansi Road ■ Open daily
At the southern end of the Nothern Ridge is one of the city's two Ashokan columns (see p51), from the reign of Ashoka (r. 269–232 BC).

Ashoka Column

Places to Eat

1 Karim's

MAP H4 ■ 16 Gali Kababiyan, Matia Mahal, Jama Masjid ■ 2326 4981 ■ Open 9am -12:45pm daily ■ ₹

This *(see p65)* Delhi institution has been doling out delicious Mughlai food for over half a century.

2 Gujarati Samaj

MAP F1 ■ 2 Raj Niwas Marg, Civil Lines ■ 2398 1796 ■ Open 6–10am, 11:30am–3pm & 7–10pm daily ■ ₹

A family-run restaurant that serves delicious, fuss-free Gujarati food.

3 Haldiram's

MAP G3 ■ 1454/2 Chandni Chowk ■ 4768 5111 ■ Open 9am–10:30pm daily ■ ₹

Good Indian street food and sweets prepared in hygienic conditions.

4 Moti Mahal

MAP H5 ■ 3703 Netaji Subhash Marg, Daryaganj ■ 2327 3661 ■ Open 11am–12:30am daily ■ ₹₹

Dating back to Independence, this restaurant claims to have invented the famous butter chicken.

5 Embassy Restaurant

MAP G1 ■ 13 Alipur Road, Civil Lines ■ 2399 3061 ■ Open noon–11:30pm daily ■ ₹₹

A delightful old-world restaurant reminiscent of Colonial clubs, serving standard North Indian fare.

6 The Curzon Room

MAP G1 ■ Oberoi Maidens, 7 Sham Nath Marg, Civil Lines ■ 2397 5464 ■ Open 7–11pm daily (buffet: 7:30–10pm) ■ ₹₹₹

Dig into the sumptuous buffet at this elegant Raj-style restaurant.

7 The Garden Terrace

MAP G1 ■ Oberoi Maidens, 7 Sham Nath Marg, Civil Lines ■ 2397 5464 ■ Open daily 7am–11pm ■ ₹₹

Spilling into a lovely courtyard, The Garden Terrace, part of the venerable Maidens Hotel, is an ideal place for nursing a cup of coffee.

8 Paranthe Wali Gali

MAP G3 ■ Opposite Natraj Restaurant, 1396 Chandni Chowk ■ Open 11am–11pm daily ■ ₹

The "alley of parantha-makers" is a real foodie's delight, offering an overwhelming variety of this delicious stuffed Indian bread.

Old-style charm at Chor Bizarre

9 Chor Bizarre

MAP H5 ■ Hotel Broadway, 4/15A Asaf Ali Road ■ 4366 3600 ■ Open noon–3pm & 7:30–11pm daily ■ ₹₹

One of the oldest restaurants in Old Delhi, Chor Bizarre *(see p64)* is famous for its superb Kashmiri cuisine.

10 Kake di Hatti

MAP G3 ■ 654 Church Mission Road, Fatehpuri, Chandni Chowk ■ 98109 09754 ■ Open 8am–1am daily ■ ₹

This place draws flocks of locals to mop up its legendary *daal makhni*.

Following pages The Diwan-i-Aam audience hall at Delhi's Red Fort

🔟 South of the Centre

The area south of New Delhi, now home to some of the city's most upmarket suburbs, boasts a superb swathe of Mughal (and some Sultanate) monuments. At the top of most visitors' lists is the magnificent Humayun's Tomb, the first great masterpiece of Mughal architecture, though there are also stand-out attractions nearby at the wonderfully atmospheric religious enclave of Nizamuddin, the beautiful parklands and historic monuments of the Lodi Gardens, Safdarjung's Tomb, and the rugged citadel of Purana Qila, while just across the Yamuna River lies Akshardham Temple, India's most extravagant modern Hindu shrine.

Khan-i-Khanan's Tomb

① Khan-i-Khanan's Tomb

MAP R7 ■ Mathura Road, south of Humayun's Tomb ■ Open sunrise–sunset daily ■ Adm

This grandiose tomb is the burial place of Abdur Rahim, Akbar's prime minister, who died in 1626, although it may have been built for his wife, who died in 1598. The tomb has four grand *iwans* and a bulbous central dome surrounded by *chattris*, rather like a sketch for the Taj Mahal minus the minarets.

SOUTH OF THE CENTRE

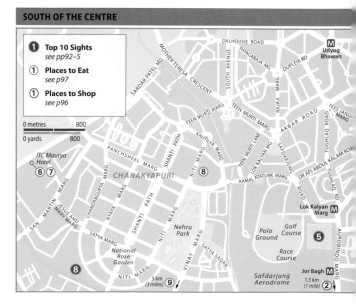

① **Top 10 Sights**
see pp92–5

① **Places to Eat**
see p97

① **Places to Shop**
see p96

0 metres 800
0 yards 800

2 Purana Qila
MAP R3 ▪ Mathura Road
▪ Pragati Maidan Metro ▪ Open
sunrise–sunset daily ▪ Adm

The sixth city of Delhi, the Purana Qila
(see p51) was begun by Humayun and
completed by his rival Sher Shah Suri.
Its large, rugged walls stretch for over
a mile and enclose a large swathe of
parkland dotted with buildings. The
most notable are the striking Qala-i-
Kuhna Masjid, and the more delicate
Sher Mandal, an unusual octagonal
pavilion that was used by Humayun
as a library and observatory.

A baby hippo at the Zoological Park

3 National Zoological Park
MAP R4 ▪ Mathura Road,
near Purana Qila ▪ Pragati Maidan
Metro ▪ Open Apr–Oct: 9am–4:30pm
Sat–Thu; Nov–Mar: 9am–4pm Sat–
Thu; closed Fri ▪ Adm ▪ www.nzp
newdelhi.gov.in

The largest of its kind in India,
Delhi's popular zoo is home to
around 2,000 animals, including
national treasures such as rhinos,
elephants and Bengal tigers, and
a good selection of wildlife from
the Americas, Australia and Africa.

Spread out over expansive parkland,
it provides a pleasant, sympathetic
environment for animals, as well
as a peaceful refuge for the city's
human population. It is also a great
spot for a weekend picnic.

4 Lodi Gardens
The beautiful Lodi Gardens
(see pp30–31) are among Delhi's most
attractive retreats, offering a beguiling
combination of nature and culture,
with an idyllic wooded landscape
dotted with fine tombs dating from
the Lodi and Sayyid dynasties.

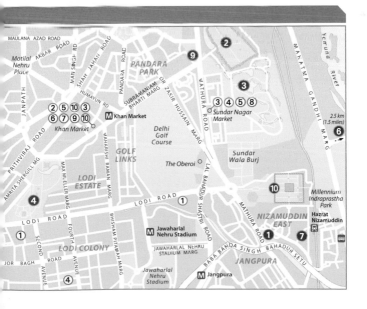

Safdarjung's Tomb, set in a *charbagh*-style garden

5 Safdarjung's Tomb

MAP M6 ■ Airforce Golf Course, at the intersection of Safdarjung Road & Aurobindo Marg ■ Taxi, auto-rickshaw or Jor Bagh Metro ■ Open sunrise–sunset daily ■ Adm

This mausoleum was built in 1754 for Safdarjung (1708–54), the Nawab of Awadh and one of the most important Mughal nobles during the reigns of Muhammad Shah and Ahmad Shah Bahadur. A good example of late-Mughal design, the tomb is a large and floridly decorated sandstone structure with a bulbous dome set in a *charbagh*-style garden.

> **LAST RITES, DELHI-STYLE**
>
> No other city in the world boasts as copious a range of mausoleums as Delhi – from certain angles the city can look like a kind of enormous necropolis. Oddly enough, such buildings run directly contrary to Koranic orthodoxy, which forbids the construction of elaborate funerary monuments – a prohibition that was ignored by the city's rulers.

6 Akshardham Temple

MAP C5 ■ Taxi or Akshardham Metro ■ Open 9:30am–6:30pm Tue–Sun ■ Electronic equipment not allowed ■ www.akshardham.com

Opened in 2005, this is perhaps the largest and most spectacular modern Hindu temple in India. The huge complex is centred on an extravagant shrine, ringed by 148 elephant statues; inside is an impressive-looking golden figure of Bhagwan Shri Swaminarayan, in whose honour the temple was built. The temple hosts exhibitions and even has a fountain water show at sunset.

7 Nizamuddin

MAP R6 ■ Taxi or Hazrat Nizamuddin Metro ■ Open 24 hrs ■ Hope Project reservations: 2435 7081 ■ Qawwali: 98117 78607; 9–10pm Thu; ■ www.nizamuddin aulia.org

This atmospheric religious enclave grew up around the tomb of the great Sufi saint Sheikh Nizamuddin Auliya (1238–1325), and is quite busy with pilgrims at all hours, with performances of devotional

Objects on sale at Nizamuddin

qawwali singing held after dark. Hope Project, a local NGO, organizes evening walking tours of the adjoining Nizamuddin village, which are a fascinating way to learn about this area.

8 National Rail Museum

MAP U1 ■ Satya Marg, Chanakyapuri ■ Dhaula Kuan Metro ■ 2688 1826 ■ Open 10am–5pm Tue–Sun ■ Adm and charge for video and train rides

The National Rail Museum is a shrine to India's fascination with all things pertaining to the train. Among the highlights are the lavish carriages of local and foreign royals, including the Prince of Wales and the Maharaja of Mysore.

Locomotive, National Rail Museum

9 Khair ul Manazil Masjid

MAP Q4 ■ Mathura Road, opposite Purana Qila ■ Pragati Maidan Metro ■ Open sunrise–sunset daily

Just across the road from the Purana Qila lies the impressive, though now rather derelict, Khair ul Manazil Masjid, built in 1562 by Maham Anga, the powerful wet-nurse of Akbar. The mosque is a classic example of early Mughal architecture, its low and rather stocky façade reminiscent of the earlier Sultanate style.

10 Humayun's Tomb

One of the greatest of all Mughal garden tombs, this superb mausoleum (see pp18–19) is one of Delhi's finest monuments and a magnificent memorial to the personable but erratic Humayun, the second Mughal emperor.

A DAY SOUTH OF THE CENTRE OF DELHI

▶ MORNING

It is possible to see most of the major sights covered in this section in one long, albeit very busy, day. Note that you will need to pick up auto-rickshaws to get between them, or hire a taxi or auto-rickshaw for the day. The highlights of the **Akshardham** temple can be seen in two hours, but for a more leisurely visit, allow half a day. Alternatively, you could pick from the following selection for a more relaxed tour.

Start your day at the imposing **Safdarjung's Tomb**, then walk a short distance down the road to the **Lodi Gardens** (see p93). Explore the various tombs that dot the beautiful parkland – don't miss the lovely bonsai garden. Relax and have lunch at the classy **Perch** (see p97) in nearby Khan Market (see p67).

AFTERNOON

Take an auto-rickshaw to the brooding **Purana Qila** (see p93), then cross the road to visit the **Khair ul Manazil Masjid**. From here, you can get another auto-rickshaw down to **Humayun's Tomb** (see p18). Explore the tomb and gardens and the other mausoleums that dot the vast complex, then walk across the road to the wonderful little *dargah* at **Nizamuddin**. For dinner, you could head to the nearby **Basil and Thyme** (see p97) in Sunder Nagar, before or after attending the evening *qawwali* session at the *dargah*.

See map on pp92–3

Places to Shop

1 The Bookshop
MAP N7 ▪ 13/7 Main Market, Jor Bagh ▪ 2469 7102

The Bookshop is lovingly stocked with a wide range of reading matter, from well-thumbed classics to pristine new arrivals.

2 Dilli Haat
MAP V1 ▪ Opposite INA Market ▪ 2611 9055 ▪ Adm

A daily open-air market run by Delhi Tourism, with several stalls selling wonderful arts and crafts – not to mention food – from every single state in India.

Amrapali bracelet

3 Good Earth
MAP P5 ▪ 9-ABC Khan Market ▪ 2464 7175

This luxurious store stocks a range of exclusively designed dining products, high-quality linen and some lovely home-decor items.

4 Mittal Tea House
MAP P7 ▪ 8-A Lodi Colony Market ▪ 2461 5709

The pleasant Mittal Tea House stocks beautifully packed Darjeeling, Assam and Nilgiri teas, as well as Kangra and Kashmiri green teas.

5 Bharany's
MAP R4 ▪ 14 Sundar Nagar Market ▪ 2435 8528

Bharany's takes pride in every one of its handcrafted jewellery items. It also has a fine collection of textiles.

6 Silverline
MAP P5 ▪ 7-A Khan Market ▪ 2464 3017

The walls of this busy shop are lined with beautiful jewellery in antique, ethnic and contemporary designs.

7 Amrapali
MAP P5 ▪ 39 Khan Market ▪ 4175 2024

The exclusive collection here includes exquisite contemporary jewellery, designer, enamel, ethnic and antique pieces.

8 Ladakh Jeweller's
MAP R4 ▪ 10 Sundar Nagar Market ▪ 2435 5424

A lovely shop that specializes in beautiful ethnic Indian handcrafted jewellery in gold and silver.

9 Ogaan Closet
MAP P5 ▪ 77 Khan Market ▪ 4175 7220

This shop has a splendid ensemble of clothes, accessories and jewellery by various Indian designers. It also provides a platform for Indian design and stocks some luxurious clothes that are exquisite in cut and design.

10 Anokhi
MAP P5 ▪ 32 Khan Market ▪ 2460 3423

Specializing in contemporary crafted textiles with roots in Jaipur, Anokhi stocks ethnic and western wear.

Anokhi's colourful designs

Places to Eat

PRICE CATEGORIES
For a meal for one, including taxes and
service charge but not alcohol.
....
₹ under ₹500 ₹₹ ₹500–1,500
₹₹₹ over ₹1,500

1 Indian Accent
MAP Q6 ■ The Lodhi,
Lodi Road ■ 6617 5151 ■ Open
noon–3:30pm, 7–9:30pm &
9:45pm–12:45am daily ■ ₹₹₹
A swanky yet cosy venue (see p64) that
offers finely prepared local dishes.

2 Perch
MAP P5 ■ 71, 1st Floor,
Khan Market ■ 83739 76637
■ Open 8am–1am daily ■ ₹₹₹
A sophisticated coffee and wine
bar with great European cuisine.
The coffee sangria is a must try.

3 Diggin
MAP V2 ■ No. 1 & 2, Siri
Fort Marg ■ 4080 0081 ■ Open
11am–11pm Mon–Fri, 8:30am–
11pm Sat & Sun ■ ₹₹
Comfy and quiet, Diggin (see p65)
is ideal for enjoying continental
meals on a lazy afternoon.

4 Basil and Thyme
MAP R4 ■ 28 Sunder Nagar
Market ■ 4378 7722 ■ Open 11am–
11pm daily ■ ₹₹
Delectable European fare is paired
with a well-curated wine list here.

5 Latitude 28
MAP P5 ■ Good Earth,
Khan Market ■ 2462 1013 ■ Open
11:30am–11:30pm daily ■ ₹₹₹
A stylish café that focuses on great
contemporary dishes with a twist.

6 Bukhara
MAP K5 ■ ITC Maurya, Sardar
Patel Marg ■ 2611 2233 ■ Open 12:30–
2:45pm & 7–11:45pm daily ■ ₹₹₹
This is one of the world's top Indian
restaurants (see p65), serving superb
North-West Frontier cuisine.

Dum Pukht's glamorous dining room

7 Dum Pukht
MAP K5 ■ ITC Maurya, Sardar
Patel Marg ■ 2611 2233 ■ Open
7–11.45pm daily; 12:30–3:45pm
Sun ■ ₹₹₹
Slow-cooked dum (steam casserole)
dishes from Lucknow, served amidst
tastefully glitzy surroundings.

8 Sagar Ratna
MAP L6 ■ The Ashok, 50-B
Chanakyapuri ■ 2688 8242 ■ Open
8am–11pm daily ■ ₹
This place serves simple, delicious
vegetarian South Indian meals.

9 Coast Café
MAP U2 ■ H-2, Hauz Khas
Village ■ 4160 1717 ■ Open noon–
1am daily ■ ₹₹
This restaurant serves curries from
coastal Kerala, fish and chicken
stews as well as delicious cocktails.

10 SodaBottleOpenerWala
MAP P5 ■ 73 Khan Market,
Subramaniam Bharti Marg ■ 98108
77701 ■ Open 8:30–12:30am daily
■ ₹₹
A quirky, old-fashioned Bombay Parsi
restaurant (see p65), successfully
re-created in Delhi.

See map on pp92–3

🔟 South Delhi

The upwardly mobile suburbs of South Delhi are where visitors will find what makes modern Delhi tick, with a string of upmarket neighbourhoods, suave restaurants and glitzy modern malls. Despite its contemporary appearance, however, South Delhi was home to the city's earliest settlements, and boasts many of its most atmospherically time-warped monuments.

Baha'i Temple

Most of these date back to the Delhi sultans, whose various forts, mosques and wonderful mausoleums still stand scattered majestically amongst modern suburbia. The highlight is the Qutb Minar complex and the adjacent Mehrauli Archaeological Park, while there are further memorable attractions at both Tughlaqabad and Hauz Khas.

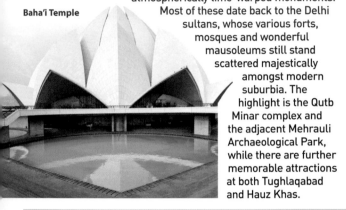

SOUTH DELHI

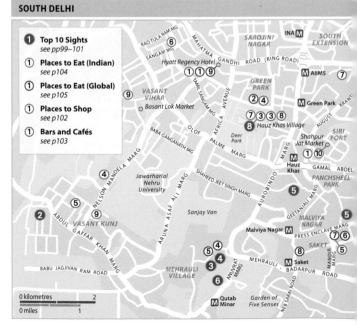

1 **Top 10 Sights**
   see pp99–101

1 **Places to Eat (Indian)**
   see p104

1 **Places to Eat (Global)**
   see p105

1 **Places to Shop**
   see p102

1 **Bars and Cafés**
   see p103

1 Baha'i Temple
MAP X2 ■ Kailash Colony
■ Open summer: 9am–6:30pm Tue–Sun; winter: 9am–5pm Tue–Sun
■ www.bahaihouseofworship.in

Completed in 1986 to a design by Iranian architect Fariborz Sahba, the Baha'i Temple is Delhi's most striking modern building. Popularly known as the Lotus Temple, the design was inspired by the image of an unfolding lotus flower, with 27 huge white petals emerging from nine pools, symbolizing the nine spiritual paths of the Baha'i faith.

2 Tomb of Sultan Ghari
MAP T3 ■ Abdul Gaffar Khan Marg, Vasant Kunj ■ Taxi or auto-rickshaw ■ Open 24 hrs

Marooned on the outskirts of the city, this impressive but little-visited tomb was built in 1231 by Iltutmish for his son and heir Nasiruddin Mahmud following the latter's premature death. It is the oldest Islamic tomb in India, looking more like a fort than a mausoleum. The name Sultan Ghari means "Royal Cave", referring to the troglodytic burial chamber beneath the central octagonal platform. The tomb is an architectural curiosity, as much Hindu as Muslim in style.

3 Quwwat-ul-Islam
The centrepiece of the Qutb Minar complex, the Quwwat-ul-Islam (see p24) was the subcontinent's first mosque, begun by Aibak and extended by his successors, including Alauddin Khilji (see p45), who added the fine Alai Darwaza red sandstone gateway in 1311. Inside, the prayer-hall screen, covered in Koranic carvings, is one of India's finest early examples of Islamic architecture.

4 Qutb Minar
One of Delhi's most iconic sights, the soaring Qutb Minar (see pp24–5) towers over the southern city: a vast minaret begun during the reign of the first Delhi sultan Qutbuddin Aibak. The design is quite unlike anything else in the subcontinent, more Afghan than Indian, with angular projecting flanges punctuated by balconies and bands of Koranic script.

Column detail at Qutb Minar

Domes at Begumpuri Masjid

5 Begumpuri and Khirki Masjids

MAP V2 ■ Off Guru Govind Singh Road ■ Hauz Khas or Malviya Nagar Metro ■ Open sunrise–sunset daily

The Begumpuri, with its arcaded courtyard topped by domes, and the Khirki, with its tapering shape and almost completely covered courtyard, are typical of the 14th-century Tughlaq era.

6 Mehrauli Village and Archaeological Park

MAP U3 ■ Anuvrat Marg, south of the Qutb Minar ■ Open sunrise–sunset daily

The Mehrauli Archaeological Park (see p27) and adjacent village of Mehrauli are home to an extraordinary collection of ancient monuments, dating from the 13th to the 19th centuries. There is a rich cluster of Mughal monuments, ranging from the Jamal-Kamali Masjid to the Zafar Mahal, and notable Sultanate-era attractions such as the Jahaz Mahal and the serene *dargah* of the Sufi saint Qutb Sahib, buried away in the depths of the village.

7 Ashoka's Rock Edict

MAP X2 ■ Off Raja Dhirsain Marg ■ Open 24 hrs

Not far from the Baha'i Temple lies a large boulder (see p51), carved with a faint tracery of fading Brahmi script. This is one of the city's three monuments dating from the time of the Mauryan Emperor Ashoka. Ashoka converted to Buddhism early in his reign, and erected, across the country, a series of pillars and rock edicts on which his various procla-mations were recorded. Unlike the city's two Ashokan columns, this rock edict stands on its original site.

8 Hauz Khas Village

MAP U2 ■ Hauz Khas Village ■ Taxi, auto-rickshaw or Green Park Metro ■ Open 24 hrs

The upmarket village of Hauz Khas is home to a string of ancient monu-ments, the Deer Park (see p58) and a number of eating and shopping venues. The village is centred around a reservoir, the Hauz-i-Alai, built by Alauddin Khilji in 1304. The sequence of buildings girding the lake was added half a century later.

Monuments at Mehrauli Village

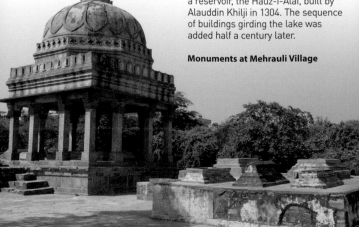

URBAN VILLAGES

Scattered amid South Delhi's suburbs are the remains of many formerly isolated villages that have now been swallowed up by the advancing urban tide. The most notable ones are Nizamuddin, Chiragh and Mehrauli. Each is home to an important *dargah* and retains its original street layout.

⑨ Chiragh Delhi
MAP W2 ■ Off Gamal Abdel Nasser Marg ■ Taxi or auto-rickshaw

Now engulfed by suburban sprawl, the ancient village of Chiragh Delhi has managed to preserve much of its traditional atmosphere, retaining parts of the walls that once surrounded it. The main attraction here is the *dargah* of Roshan Chiragh Delhi, while the tomb of Delhi sultan, Buhlul Lodi, lies outside the village.

Citadel ruins at Tughlaqabad

⑩ Tughlaqabad
MAP X3 ■ Mehrauli-Badarpur Road ■ Taxi, auto-rickshaw or Badarpur Border Metro ■ Open sunrise–sunset daily ■ Adm and charge for video

Constructed during the reign of Ghiyasuddin Tughlaq, Tughlaqabad (*see p50*) was the third city of Delhi, dwarfing the previous settlements of Siri and Lal Kot, with a string of fortified ramparts and city walls stretching for 6 km (4 miles). The walls and citadel within are now largely ruined, but still impressive and worth a visit. Just over the road lies the austere tomb of Ghiyasuddin himself.

A DAY IN SOUTH DELHI

▶ MORNING

South Delhi's attractions are spread out, and you will need to take transport between the various sites. You could pick up auto-rickshaws between each stop, though it is easiest to hire a knowledgeable taxi- or auto-rickshaw-driver for the day to ferry you around.

Start the day with an hour or so at the remarkable **Qutb Minar Complex** (*see p99*) and spend the rest of the morning exploring the monuments of the **Mehrauli Archaeological Park** and the adjacent **Mehrauli Village**. Next, head to the excellent **Garden of Five Senses** (*see p58*) and have lunch at **Olive Bar & Kitchen** (*see p105*).

AFTERNOON

After lunch, head north, taking in some of Delhi's least-visited but most absorbing monuments, including the **Begumpuri Masjid**. Stop in the fascinating urban village of **Chiragh Delhi** to visit the *dargah*. If you have time, go to the **Khirki Masjid** and nearby **Lal Gumbad** (*see p44*). Then, drive over towards Hauz Khas. Visit the beautiful reservoir and surrounding buildings, the Deer Park, and then explore the quiet streets of **Hauz Khas Village** and its superb boutique shops. Continue north to the **Baha'i Temple** (*see p99*), aiming to arrive in the evening when the lighting makes it look spectacular. Finally, make your way back to Nehru Place to the International Trade Tower for a meal at **Oh! Calcutta** (*see p104*).

See map on pp98–9

Places to Shop

① Shahpur Jat Market
MAP V2 ■ Shahpur Jat, Siri Fort ■ Open daily (timings vary)

Vintage and contemporary clothing, accessories, jewellery, rugs and home decor are all on offer in the trendy new fashion boutiques of this chic urban village.

② Kilol
MAP W2 ■ 4-N Block Market, Greater Kailash I ■ 2924 3388 ■ Open 10:30am–8pm daily

A lovely store specializing in hand-block-printed, reasonably priced fabrics from Jaipur.

③ Tatsat
MAP U2 ■ E-50 Main Market, Hauz Khas ■ 4165 5792 ■ Open 10am–8pm Mon–Sat, noon–8pm Sun

Tatsat sells garments, accessories, recycled goods, stationery and colourful hand-painted *chai* glasses and kettles, all sourced from eco-friendly organizations.

④ DLF Emporio
MAP T2 ■ 4 Nelson Mandela Marg, Vasant Kunj ■ 4611 6666 ■ Open 11am–9pm daily

Delhi's most deluxe shopping mall, where affluent Delhiites come to buy designerwear from all the top international brands.

⑤ Ravissant
MAP X1 ■ 50–51 Community Centre, New Friends Colony ■ 2683 7278 ■ Open 10am–7pm Mon–Sat ■ www.ravissant.in

A sophisticated store with beautiful "Indian-inspired" clothes in breezy fabrics, home decor and silverware.

⑥ Abraham & Thakore
MAP W1 ■ Moonriver Building, D-16 Defence Colony ■ 98717 74436 ■ Open 10:30am–7pm Mon–Sat ■ www.abrahamandthakore.com

A Delhi fashion institution best known for its classic cuts and pristine natural fabrics.

⑦ Nalli
MAP V1 ■ D-2 South Extension II ■ 2462 9926 ■ Open 10am–8:30pm daily

Established in 1928, Nalli is popular for its traditional silk saris.

⑧ Utsav
MAP W2 ■ 3 Krishi Vihar Complex ■ 2624 2420 ■ Open 11am–7:30pm Mon–Sat

Utsav stocks saris in every possible fabric imaginable, plus accessories.

Exquisite Fabindia furnishings

⑨ Fabindia
MAP W2 ■ 7-N Block Market, Greater Kailash I ■ 4669 3706 ■ Open 10am–8pm daily

Fabindia stocks everything from furniture and natural cosmetics to organic food and clothes.

⑩ Zaza
MAP W2 ■ 25–26 Community Centre, Zamrudpur ■ 4105 2525 ■ Open 10am–8pm daily

A lovely lifestyle store filled with beautiful furniture, brightly coloured linen, unusual cutlery and covetable home decor products.

Bars and Cafés

1 **Polo Lounge**
MAP U1 ■ Hyatt Regency,
Bhikaji Cama Place ■ 6677 1314
■ Open 11am–1am daily
Step back in time at this plush,
England-inspired bar.

2 **Cirrus 9**
MAP R5 ■ The Oberoi,
Dr Zakir Hussain Marg ■ 2436
3030 ■ Open 5pm–1am
The rooftop bar (see p65) at the Oberoi
Hotel offers views of the Delhi Golf
Course and Humayun's Tomb.

3 **Social**
MAP U2 ■ 9-A & 12, Hauz
Khas Village ■ 78386 52814
■ Open 11am–1am daily
A popular restaurant-bar, Social
(see p65) serves a range of global
dishes, creative cocktails and some
of the best breakfasts in Delhi.

4 **The Piano Man**
MAP V2 ■ B-6-7/22 Safdarjung
Enclave Market ■ 4131 5181 ■ Open
noon–12:45am daily
This club, with a grand piano and an
intimate bar, is a great place for live
jazz performances and cocktails.

5 **Monkey Bar**
MAP T2 ■ Plot 11 Upper
Ground Floor, LSC, Pocket C-6 & 7,
Vasant Kunj ■ 4109 5155 ■ Open
noon–12:30am daily
A hip new bar with a touch of the
gastropub and great cocktails.

6 **Lord of the Drinks Forum**
MAP W2 ■ Epicuria Mall, Nehru
Place Metro Station ■ 85888 44116
■ Open noon–12:30am daily
With great ambiance and incredible
music, this place offers a selection
of innovative drinks and cocktails.

7 **Shalom**
MAP W2 ■ 10-N Block
Market, Greater Kailash I ■ 98100
48084 ■ Open noon–1am daily
Live music, paired with cool
Mediterranean decor and great
cocktails, make Shalom one of the
city's most popular nightclubs.

8 **Kunzum Travel Café**
MAP V2 ■ T-49, Hauz Khas
Village ■ 96507 02777 ■ Open
11am–7:30pm Tue–Sun
This unique café is a great place to
chat with fellow travel enthusiasts
over a cup of coffee.

9 **PCO**
MAP T3 ■ 4-D Block Market,
Vasant Vihar ■ 4606 2444 ■ Open
5:30pm–12:30am daily
A "speakeasy", with a secret entry
code, retro decor and exotic cocktails.

10 **Café Turtle**
MAP W2 ■ 16 N Block Market,
Greater Kailash I ■ 2924 5641
■ Open 10:30am–8:30pm daily
A relaxed, friendly café atop the
lovely Full Circle bookstore.

People enjoying coffee amidst books at Café Turtle

See map on pp98–9

Places to Eat (Indian)

1 Swagath
MAP W1 ▪ 14 Main Market, Defence Colony ▪ 2433 0930 ▪ Open 11am–midnight daily ▪ ₹₹
Swagath is known for serving some of the most delicious South Indian fare in town.

2 Oh! Calcutta
MAP W2 ▪ Ground floor, International Trade Tower, Nehru Place ▪ 2646 4182 ▪ Open 12:30–3:30pm & 7:30–11:15pm daily ▪ ₹₹
Exuding old-world charm, this restaurant specializes in excellent traditional Bengali fare.

3 Carnatic Café
MAP X1 ▪ Community Centre, New Friends Colony ▪ 4100 8630 ▪ Open 9am–10:30pm daily ▪ ₹
Innovative dosas and fabulous filter coffee served at reasonable prices.

4 Sagar
MAP W1 ▪ 18 Defence Colony Market ▪ 2433 3658 ▪ Open 8am–11pm daily ▪ ₹
A friendly canteen-style place, with reasonably priced, delicious vegetarian South Indian cuisine.

5 Dakshin
MAP V3 ▪ Sheraton New Delhi Hotel, District Centre, Saket ▪ 4266 1122 ▪ Open 12:30–2:45pm & 7:30–11:45pm daily ▪ ₹₹₹
Elegant and unassuming, this place serves the best Malayali food in the city.

6 Delhi Club House
MAP U1 ▪ Sangam Courtyard, R K Puram ▪ 97175 35533 ▪ Open noon–12:30am daily ▪ ₹₹
This restaurant-bar offers a curated selection of signature dishes from clubhouses across India.

The colourful entrance to Naivedyam

7 Naivedyam
MAP U2 ▪ Hauz Khas Village ▪ Open10am–10:30pm ▪ 4175 4984 ▪ ₹
Known for its cosy ambience and quick service, this place offers South Indian cuisine on a budget.

8 Juggernaut
MAP W2 ▪ HS-16, Kailash Colony Market ▪ 4131 9991 ▪ Open 6am–11pm daily ▪ ₹
With its fun, unconventional decor and innovative menu, this place has become popular with the local crowd for delicious South Indian meals.

9 Fabcafe
MAP T3 ▪ Shop 10, Sector B, Vasant Kunj ▪ 3310 6192 ▪ Open 8:30am–11pm daily ▪ ₹₹
A product of Fabindia *(see p102)*, this modern Indian bistro is all about locally-grown organic produce, and even offers a vegan menu.

Authentic Malayali cuisine at Dakshin

10 Potbelly Rooftop Cafe
MAP V2 ▪ 116-C, 4th Floor, Shahpur Jat ▪ 4161 2048 ▪ Open 12:30–11pm daily ▪ ₹
The authentic Bihari cuisine served at this rooftop restaurant includes *litti chokha* – a roasted dough ball stuffed with *sattu* (roasted chickpea flour), served with mashed roast aubergine and potato.

Places to Eat (Global)

PRICE CATEGORIES

For a meal for one, inclusive of taxes and service charge but not alcohol.

₹ under ₹500 ₹₹ ₹500–1,500
₹₹₹ over ₹1,500

1 The China Kitchen
MAP U1 ■ Hyatt Regency, Bhikaji Cama Place ■ 6677 1334 ■ Open noon–2:30pm Mon–Fri, noon–3:30pm Sat & Sun, 7–11:30pm daily ■ ₹₹₹

A culinary milestone for Chinese food in the city, the food here *(see p65)* is complemented with stylish interiors.

2 Hyjack Restaurant and Bar
MAP V2 ■ B-6/6 DDA Market, opposite Deer Park, Safdarjung Enclave ■ 4604 9801 ■ Open 11am–1am daily ■ ₹

With seating on the terrace and an amazing view of the Deer Park *(see p58)*, Hyjack offers Pan Asian and European cuisine and good cocktails.

3 Diva
MAP W2 ■ M-8A, M Block Market, Greater Kailash II ■ 2921 5673 ■ Open 12:30–4pm & 7–11:30pm daily ■ ₹₹

This quiet, understated restaurant serves arguably the best Italian food in town. Sunday brunch is popular.

4 Qla
MAP U3 ■ 4-A, Seven Style Mile, Kalka Das Marg, Kila, Mehrauli ■ 3007 9200 ■ Open noon–midnight Wed–Mon ■ ₹₹₹

This fine-dining restaurant serves European-influenced cuisine in an old *haveli* (mansion). The courtyard is ideal for sunny brunches and atmospheric dinners.

5 Olive Bar & Kitchen
MAP U3 ■ One Style Mile, Haveli 6, Mehrauli ■ 2957 4444 ■ Open 12:30am–12:30pm daily ■ ₹₹₹

Set in a *haveli*, Olive *(see p64)* offers light Italian and Mediterranean fare.

6 Burma Burma
MAP V3 ■ S-25, Select Citywalk, Saket ■ 4914 5807 ■ Open noon–4pm & 6:30–11pm Mon–Thu, noon–11pm Fri–Sun ■ ₹₹

Enjoy contemporary Burmese cuisine along with a selection of teas here.

7 Smoke House Deli
MAP U2 ■ 252/253, DLF Place Mall, Saket ■ 78385 20899 ■ Open 10:30–1am daily ■ ₹₹

A modern European restaurant, that focuses on smoked and grilled meats.

8 Lebanese Point
MAP V3 ■ Shop 7 Ground Floor, PVR Anupam Shopping Complex, Saket ■ 4166 4440 ■ Open 1–11:30pm daily ■ ₹

The best chicken shawarmas in town; decent falafel and mezze, too.

9 La Piazza
MAP U1 ■ Hyatt Regency ■ 6677 1310 ■ Open 11:45am–3pm Mon–Fri, 11:45am–3:30pm Sat & Sun, 6:45–11:30pm daily ■ ₹₹

Fresh, hearty Italian dishes are served here amid relaxed surroundings.

10 Fio Cookhouse & Bar
MAP W2 ■ Epicuria Mall, Nehru Place Metro Station ■ 99710 04536 ■ Open 12:30pm–12:30am daily ■ ₹₹₹

European and Indian cuisine, plus inventive cocktails are on offer here.

The stylish interiors at Fio

Top 10 Delhi
Streetsmart

Auto-rickshaws parked in New Delhi

Getting To and Around Delhi

Arriving by Air

The city's **Indira Gandhi International Airport** has two main terminals – T3 handles international and some domestic flights (carriers include **Air India**, **Air Canada**, **Jet Airways**, **British Airways**, **Virgin Atlantic** and **United Airlines**), and T1 is used for low-cost domestic flights (airlines include **IndiGo**, **SpiceJet** and **Go Air**). Some domestic carriers, such as **Vistara**, fly out of T3. A third terminal, T2, will be in operation temporarily while T1 undergoes refurbishment. There are direct flights to Delhi from all major hubs, including London, Toronto, New York, and Sydney.

The fastest way into town from T3 is via the Airport Express Link (5am–11pm) of the Delhi Metro, which takes 20 minutes to reach New Delhi rail station (Ajmeri Gate side). From T1 there's a connecting shuttle (6am–10pm) to Delhi Aerocity station.

A 24-hour bus service connects both terminals to Connaught Place, New Delhi Station (Ajmeri Gate side), the Red Fort and Maharana Pratap ISBT (40 minutes). All three terminals are connected via a 24x7 inter-terminal bus service.

For taxis, there are pre-paid taxi kiosks in the arrivals area, but prices vary, so check a few.

Arriving by Train

The most convenient train station for visitors is New Delhi, which, despite its name, is located between New Delhi and Old Delhi. Some services from northern India use Delhi Junction at the northern end of Old Delhi. Many from the south (including some from Agra) use Hazrat Nizamuddin, south of the centre near Nizamuddin village, while those from the east may terminate at Anand Vihar, and those from Rajasthan terminate at Sarai Rohilla.

New Delhi and Anand Vihar have metro stations. Delhi Junction is served by Chandni Chowk metro. There is a metro station at Hazrat Nizamuddin. All rail terminals have kiosks for pre-paid auto-rickshaw fares.

For the city of Agra, the most convenient service is the 6am Bhopal Shatabdi Express from New Delhi, returning from Agra Cantonment station at 9:15pm.

Stations are a hotspot for theft; always keep an eye on your baggage, and beware of anyone trying to distract your attention.

Foreign tourists should buy their tickets from the **Foreigners' Booking Office** on the upper floor of New Delhi station (bring your passport). Staff can advise on the best trains to use, or you can check the **Indian Railways** website for timetables or call the **Railway Enquiries** phone number. Ignore anyone who tells you that the office has closed or volunteers directions to it (almost certainly with the intention of directing you to a crooked travel agent).

Arriving by Road

The main intercity bus station is **Maharana Pratap ISBT** (Intercity State Bus Terminal) in Old Delhi, served by the Kashmiri Gate metro station. Some use **Anand Vihar ISBT** (Anand Vihar metro station), while **Rajasthan Roadways** buses arrive at Bikaner House near India Gate.

Travelling by Metro and Bus

The **Delhi Metro**, which runs from 5am until midnight, is the most convenient way of getting around town. Trains run every two to four minutes, and tickets are cheap. Rechargeable Smart Cards save time and are worth getting if you intend to use the metro during your trip. The one-day Tourist Card is not good value. Women have reserved seats, as well as the first carriage to themselves, which is a good option to use during peak hours. Baggage is limited to 15 kg (33 lb), or 60 cm x 45 cm x 25 cm (23.5 in x 17.5 in x 10 in).

DTC (Delhi Transport Corporation) has a good bus network. Routes can be confusing, and vehicles may be very crowded, but at times the service can be very handy. Their website can tell you the best route between any two stops, but you will need to know their correct names. "One", a common mobility card, can be used for both Metro and DTC buses, and can be found at all metro stations.

Travelling by Taxi

Your hotel should be able to book you a cab, but otherwise it's best to hire one from a local stand. Metered radio cabs are a good option, but they cost a little more – **Meru Cabs**, **Mega Cabs**, and **Quick Cabs** can be booked online, by phone, or via their apps. You can book taxis online through apps such as **Ola** and **Uber**.

Travelling by Auto-Rickshaw

Auto-rickshaws ("autos") are the standard way of getting around Delhi. They are fitted with meters, but most drivers won't use them and you may have to haggle. Know what price you want to pay before stopping an auto, and agree on a fare before setting off. Fares should be ₹25 for the first two kilometres then roughly ₹8 per kilometre. You can avoid haggling (and ensure you don't get overcharged) by hiring pre-paid autos at official set rates from kiosks in Connaught Place, at Janpath (outside the tourism office) and at major transport terminals.

Travelling by Cycle Rickshaw

Cycle rickshaws are a great way to get around the old city. Fares are about half those of an auto, but again, haggling is the order of the day. These are banned from Connaught Place and central New Delhi. *Rickshawwallahs* are some of Delhi's poorest: if they do a good job, be generous.

Travelling on Foot

While some pockets of the city are good for exploring on foot, it is best if you are aware of their surroundings at all times. Honking on roads is very common so don't be alarmed. Look to either side of the road before crossing as people often drive on the wrong side. Major roads have footover bridges and underpasses (subways), so make sure to use them when possible.

DIRECTORY

ARRIVING BY AIR

Air Canada
📞 4717 2900
🌐 aircanada.com

Air India
📞 1 800 180 1407
🌐 airindia.in

British Airways
📞 0124 412 0715
🌐 britishairways.com

Go Air
📞 1860 210 0999
🌐 goair.in

IndiGo
📞 0124 617 3838
🌐 goindigo.in

Indira Gandhi International Airport
📞 0124 337 6000
🌐 newdelhiairport.in

Jet Airways
📞 3989 3333
🌐 jetairways.com

SpiceJet
📞 98718 03333
🌐 spicejet.com

United Airlines
📞 0124 431 5500
🌐 united.com

Virgin Atlantic
📞 0124 469 3030
🌐 virgin-atlantic.com

Vistara
📞 92892 28888
🌐 airvistara.com

ARRIVING BY TRAIN

Foreigners' Booking Office
New Delhi Railway Station, Upper Floor;
8am–8pm Mon–Sat, 8am–2pm Sun
📞 2334 6804

Indian Railways
🌐 indianrail.gov.in

Railway Enquiries
📞 2336 6177
🌐 enquiry.indianrail. gov.in/ntes

ARRIVING BY ROAD

Anand Vihar ISBT
📞 2215 2431

Maharana Pratap ISBT
📞 2386 8694

Rajasthan Roadways
Bikaner House
📞 2338 3469

TRAVELLING BY METRO AND BUS

Delhi Metro
📞 2341 7910
🌐 delhimetrorail.com

DTC
📞 1 800 118 181
🌐 dtcbusroutes.in

TRAVELLING BY TAXI

Mega Cabs
📞 90909 09090
🌐 megacabs.com

Meru Cabs
📞 4422 4422
🌐 merucabs.com

Ola
🌐 olacabs.com

Quick Cabs
📞 6767 6767
🌐 quickcabservices.co.in

Uber
🌐 uber.com/cities/ new-delhi

Practical Information

Passports and Visas

Everybody (except those from Nepal and Bhutan) needs a visa to enter India. Nationals of most countries, if arriving at Delhi airport with an onward or return ticket, can get a 30-day tourist **e-Visa** online before their departure. For a longer stay, you'll need to apply in person or by post at the nearest **Visa Office** or alternatively at the Indian High Commission – there is a list of the latter on the website of the **Ministry of External Affairs**. It's best to allow plenty of time. Your passport should be valid for at least six months beyond your arrival date. The **UK, US, Canada, Australia, New Zealand** and many other countries have consular representation in the city.

Customs and Immigration

Duty-free limits are two litres of liquor, and 100 cigarettes or 25 cigars or 125 g (4 oz) tobacco.

Travel Safety Advice

Visitors can get up-to-date travel safety information from the **UK Foreign** and **Commonwealth Office**, the **US Department of State** and the **Australian Department of Foreign Affairs and Trade**.

Travel Insurance

Don't travel without valid insurance, and check the details of the policy for how much you can claim for the loss of individual items. For medical treatment you may have to pay first and claim it back later.

Health

Vaccinations against meningitis, typhoid, tetanus and hepatitis A are commonly recommended for India. Make sure that you are covered against polio. Exactly what you need will depend on where you are going, so consult your doctor before your trip. Malaria and dengue fever outbreaks can occur, especially in and after the monsoon months (July–September), so bring high-DEET repellent and protect yourself against mosquito bites.

Stick to bottled drinking water (or purify your own) and avoid food left lying out – the busier and more popular the restaurant, the safer it is likely to be. Street food can play havoc with those who have delicate constitutions, and ice cream, salads, juices and fruit are all germ-carriers. The most common tourist illness is "Delhi belly" – a stomach upset that passes within a day or two (stick to water, yoghurt and rice). If your symptoms persist, it's a good idea to consult a doctor, in case it's giardia or amoebic dysentery. **AIIMS** (All India Institute of Medical Sciences) is one of the country's top research hospitals; other hospitals include **Dr Ram Manohar Lohia Hospital**, the **East West Medical Centre**, and chains such as **Apollo Hospitals** and **Max Healthcare**. The **US Embassy Delhi Doctors List** is useful. The **Apollo Pharmacy** in Connaught Place is open 24 hours.

Personal Security

Violent crime against tourists is rare, but petty theft is quite common, as is credit-card fraud. If you are paying with a card, ensure that it is swiped in front of you and never leaves your sight.

Transport terminals are hotspots for theft. There have been cases of travellers being given drugged food or drink and then robbed, so never accept either from strangers.

Most hotels have a safe for valuables, although it is not unknown for things to go missing from cheap hotels. Use your own padlock to lock your baggage or even the room.

Sexual harassment of women ("eve teasing") is unfortunately quite rife. It is best to point out the perpetrator and explain in a loud voice exactly what he has done, as other people will be on your side. Violent attacks on women occasionally occur, so exercise caution after dark. Dressing conservatively may help. When hiring a car or taxi, make sure to note the licence plate number. Use "ladies' lines" when you need to queue for anything. There are "ladies only" seats or compartments on many buses and metro trains.

LGBT+ travellers should note that India is a conservative country, so it is best to avoid public displays of affection.

Emergency Services

To contact the police, call their Tourist Helpline or the **Women's Helpline**; the tourist police also have posts at the airport, main stations, major tourist sights and hotel areas. There are dedicated numbers for the **ambulance**, **fire brigade** and **police**.

Travellers with Specific Needs

The city isn't accessible for the disabled, but things are improving. Old Delhi is especially hard-going in a wheelchair. New Delhi, with its wider pavements (and cow ban) is easier. The airport and metro stations are accessible. Major sights such as the National Museum, Crafts Museum, Qutb Minar and the Red Fort make some effort, with ramps and accessible toilets. HoHo tour buses *(see p109)* are accessible and some buses with lifts have been added to the DTC fleet.

Currency and Banking

The local currency is rupees (₹), which come in notes of ₹2,000, ₹500, ₹200, ₹100, ₹50, ₹20, ₹10 and occasionally still ₹5, with coins of ₹10, ₹5, ₹2, ₹1 and 50 paise. It is illegal to import or export Indian currency. If you have over US$10,000 in foreign currency, you must declare it.

Banks are open from 10am to mid-afternoon Monday to Friday, plus a couple of hours on Saturday mornings. Private bureaux de change are becoming quite common, especially in Connaught Place and Paharhanj, and may offer decent rates. Mid- and upper-range hotels exchange foreign currency, but often at poor rates. ATMs are common and accept foreign issued credit and debit cards (especially MasterCard and Visa). These are widely accepted in upmarket shops and restaurants, but may have an extra charge.

DIRECTORY

PASSPORTS AND VISAS

Australia
🔲 india.embassy.gov.au

Canada
🔲 india.gc.ca

e-Visa
🔲 indianvisaonline.gov.in

Ministry of External Affairs
🔲 mea.gov.in

New Zealand
🔲 nzembassy.com/india

UK
🔲 ukinindia.fco.gov.uk

US
🔲 in.usembassy.gov

Visa Office, Australia
🔲 vfsglobal.com/india/australia

Visa Office, Canada
🔲 blsindia-canada.com

Visa Office, UK
🔲 vfsglobal.com/India/UK

Visa Office, US
🔲 in.ckgs.us

TRAVEL SAFETY ADVICE

Australian Department of Foreign Affairs and Trade
🔲 dfat.gov.au
🔲 smartraveller.gov.au

UK Foreign and Commonwealth Office
🔲 gov.uk/foreign-travel advice

US Department of State
🔲 travel.state.gov

HEALTH

AIIMS
Aurobindo Marg
📞 6590 0669
🔲 aiims.edu

Apollo Hospitals
🔲 apollohospdelhi.com

Apollo Pharmacy
G-8 Connaught Place
📞 2371 1838

Dr Ram Manohar Lohia Hospital
Baba Kharak Singh Marg
📞 2340 4286
🔲 rmlh.nic.in

East West Medical Centre
38 Golf Links
📞 2469 9229
🔲 eastwestrescue.com

Max Healthcare
📞 4055 4055
🔲 maxhealthcare.in

US Embassy Delhi Doctors List
🔲 in.usembassy.gov/u-s-citizen-services/local-resources-of-u-s-citizens/doctors

EMERGENCY SERVICES

Ambulance
📞 102

Fire Brigade
📞 101

Police
📞 100 or 1090

Tourist Helpline
📞 87508 71111

Women's Helpline
📞 1091

Telephone and Internet

International and national calls can be made easily and relatively cheaply from telephone booths (look for places advertising STD/ISD phone calls). Calls can often be made from hotel rooms, but there may be a mark-up, so check rates first. The country code for India is +91; the area code for Delhi is 011.

If you are planning to use your mobile in Delhi, check rates and accessibility with your service provider at home. Alternatively, buy a local SIM card (available at phone shops), for an Indian telephone number.

Most hotels provide Wi-Fi access, and many bars and cafés provide free Wi-Fi, there are also a few free Wi-Fi zones in the city. For internet cafés try **Sunrise** and **Cyber Floor** at Connaught Place.

Postal Services

There is a branch of the **Post Office** at Connaught Place. For poste restante, you will need to go to the **General Post Office** (GPO), near Connaught Place. Sending letters and postcards is easy, but packages do need to be sealed.

TV, Radio and Newspapers

Most hotel rooms in Delhi have a TV with local and international channels. Local FM radio stations, including **Zabardast Hit FM**, **Red FM**, **Radio City** and **Radio Mirchi**, play mostly Hindi pop; **Radio One** plays a more international selection. The national radio station,

All India Radio, has three daily news bulletins in English, and the **BBC World Service** can be picked up in the evenings.

India's English-language press includes *The Times of India* (whose local edition has the useful Delhi Times supplement) and *Hindustan Times*, *The Hindu*, and the *Indian Express*. **India Today** is an English-language television network that is broadcast 24 hours a day.

Opening Hours

Shops typically open 10am–6pm Monday to Saturday. Many museums and some tourist sights are closed on Mondays.

Time Difference

Delhi is on India Standard Time (IST), which is 5.5 hours ahead of London, 9.5 hours ahead of New York, 12.5 hours ahead of Los Angeles, and 4.5 hours behind Sydney.

Electrical Appliances

The electricity supply is 230V 50Hz AC. Most sockets are triple round-pin but take European-size double round-pin plugs. British, Irish and Australasian devices will only need an adaptor. North American devices will need an adaptor and a converter.

Weather

Visit in spring (February–April) or autumn (mid-September–November). Delhi is extremely hot in May and June (reaching 45°C/113°F), rather wet from late June until

mid-September, when monsoon kicks in, and chilly in December and January, when temperatures can dip below 5°C (41°F).

Visitor Information

India Tourism and **Delhi Tourism** have offices off Connaught Place, and Delhi Tourism has offices at the airport and bus and train stations.

Delhi Diary, free at the India Tourism office, lists exhibitions and cultural events, while **Time Out Delhi** has entertainment listings. Online, check out **Delhi Capital**, **Little Black Book** and **India for You**.

Trips and Tours

DTTDC runs a range of tours in town and out, including a one-day city tour, and DTC also runs one-day city tours by bus. **HoHo** has hop-on hop-off bus tours, and **Delhi by Cycle** runs 3.5-hour cycle tours. Organizations such as **Delhi Heritage Walks** and **Delhi Food Walks** offer guided walking tours.

Shopping

Crafts from all over India are available in Delhi. The State Emporia Complex *(see p67)* has fixed prices and is the best place to start looking. The Crafts Museum shop *(see pp28–9)* and Dilli Haat *(see p96)* have excellent selections. They are worth visiting to check prices and quality before heading elsewhere. Bargaining is de rigueur in bazaars and most small shops, but not usually in malls and government emporiums.

Delhi is great for clothes, from upmarket but affordable local chains such as Fabindia (see p102) and Anokhi (see p96) to bargain offerings in bazaars such as Katra Neel (see p67).

Hundreds of shops sell textiles by the metre. Buy some fabric and have your clothes tailored.

Other top buys include accessories such as belts, bags and jewellery; home decor; natural cosmetics; tea and spices, especially at Khari Baoli market (see p66); books (the city has excellent bookshops); and Bollywood film posters, which curio shops in Hauz Khas Village (see p67) have at bargain prices.

Dining

Delhi has a vibrant food scene with vegetarians well catered for. The Indian staple of *paneer* (cottage cheese) is a good alternative to meat in curries. Be sure to sample Mughlai cuisine in Agra, largely non-vegetarian, with creamy, delicate sauces, dried fruit and nuts. In south Indian restaurants, a *thali* is a good option, consisting of a selection of curries plus rice and breads. Majnu ka Tila (see p60) is a great place for Tibetan food.

Most restaurants, such as Haldiram's (see p89), are child-friendly. If kids find spicy food hard to deal with, there are many alternatives including cafés, international chains and multi-cuisine restaurants among others.

Accommodation

Delhi has a huge range of accommodation, from five-star hotels to cheap backpacker lodges. Rates for mid-range accommodation are a bargain by Western standards. **Airbnb** is very useful for locating unique places to stay. **Couchsurfing**, which allows travellers to book to stay with a family for a short period, is also available in Delhi.

DIRECTORY

TELEPHONE AND INTERNET

Cyber Floor
17 Scindia House, Connaught Place
📞 85859 78587

Sunrise
N-9/2, Connaught Place
📞 92129 35568

POSTAL SERVICES

General Post Office
Patel Chowk on Sansad Marg at Ashoka Road

Post Office
A-6 Connaught Place;
10am–7pm Mon–Sat

TV, RADIO AND NEWSPAPERS

All India Radio
1368kHz MW
🖥 allindiaradio.gov.in

BBC World Service
1413kHz MW

Hindustan Times
🖥 hindustantimes.com

Indian Express
🖥 indianexpress.com

India Today
🖥 indiatoday.com

Radio City
91.1MHz FM
🖥 planetradiocity.com

Radio Mirchi
98.3MHz FM
🖥 radiomirchi.com

Radio One
94.3MHz FM
🖥 radioone.in

Red FM
93.5MHz FM
🖥 redfmindia.in/delhi

The Hindu
🖥 thehindu.com

The Times of India
🖥 timesofindia.com

Zabardast Hit FM
95.0MHz FM
🖥 hit95fm.in

VISITOR INFORMATION

Delhi Capital
🖥 delhicapital.com

Delhi Diary
🖥 delhidiary.in

Delhi Tourism
Coffee Home, Baba Kharak Singh Marg
🖥 delhitourism.gov.in

India for You
🖥 indfy.com/delhi

India Tourism
88 Janpath
🖥 incredibleindia.org

Little Black Book
🖥 lbb.in/delhi

Time Out Delhi
🖥 timeout.com/delhi

TRIPS AND TOURS

Delhi by Cycle
🖥 delhibycycle.com

Delhi Food Walks
🖥 delhifoodwalks.com

Delhi Heritage Walks
🖥 delhiheritagewalks.com

DTC
🖥 dtc.nic.in

DTTDC
📞 2336 3607

HoHo
🖥 hohodelhi.com

ACCOMMODATION

Airbnb
🖥 airbnb.com

Couchsurfing
🖥 couchsurfing.com

Places to Stay

PRICE CATEGORIES
For a standard, double room per night (with breakfast if included), taxes and extra charges.
....
₹ under ₹5,000   ₹₹ ₹5,000–15,000   ₹₹₹ over ₹15,000

Luxury Hotels

The Claridges
MAP N5 ■ 12 Dr APJ Abdul Kalam Road ■ 3955 5000 ■ www.claridges.com/hotels/the-claridges-new-delhi ■ ₹₹
A landmark in Lutyens's Delhi, Claridges is the epitome of old-world style. The building, with Colonial-style pillars and high ceilings, has 137 rooms and suites as well as great restaurants. The Beatles stayed here in 1968.

Hyatt Regency
MAP U1 ■ Bhikaji Cama Place ■ 2679 1234 ■ www.delhi.regency.hyatt.com ■ ₹₹
The Hyatt is ideal for those who like to feel the pulse of the city. The imposing structure has stylish and spacious rooms, a sleek club lounge and some excellent restaurants.

The Lalit
MAP G6 ■ Barakhamba Avenue, Connaught Place ■ 4444 7777 ■ www.thelalit.com ■ ₹₹
Rooms are stylish and modern at this sleek five-star a few minutes away from Connaught Place. It is home to the chic nightclub Kitty Su (see p82).

The Park
MAP F7 ■ 15 Parliament Street ■ 2374 3000 ■ www.theparkhotels.com ■ ₹₹
Contemporary art and design are the highlight of this hotel's decor, but the impeccable service and chic, spacious rooms are welcome additions. Unwind at Aqua (see p82), which is set around a swimming pool.

The Imperial
MAP F7 ■ 1 Janpath ■ 2344 1234 ■ www.theimperialindia.com ■ ₹₹₹
Opened in 1931, the Imperial is considered one of Asia's finest hotels. From its sweeping palm-lined drive to its classical white Colonial structure, the place exudes quiet elegance and luxury. The walls are lined with a fine collection of European "traveller" paintings.

ITC Maurya
MAP K4 ■ Diplomatic Enclave, Sardar Patel Marg ■ 2611 2233 ■ www.itchotels.in ■ ₹₹₹
Nestled in greenery, this is a delightful accommodation option due to its impeccable service, location, forested Ridge views and excellent restaurant, Bukhara (see p65). It also houses beautiful artworks from eminent artists.

The Lodhi
MAP Q6 ■ Lodi Road ■ 4363 3333 ■ www.thelodhi.com ■ ₹₹₹
The Lodhi combines modern decor with traditional touches such as Lodi-inspired *jali* screens and *Khareda* stone floors. The hotel has a great spa with Turkish *hammam* and private pools. The suites offer excellent views.

The Oberoi
MAP Q4 ■ Dr Zakir Hussain Marg ■ 2436 3030 ■ www.oberoihotels.com ■ ₹₹₹
The Oberoi features rooms and suites inspired by the designs of Lutyens' New Delhi. It also offers views of the Delhi Golf Course and Humayun's Tomb (see p95).

Oberoi Maidens
MAP G1 ■ 7 Sham Nath Marg ■ 2397 5464 ■ www.maidenshotel.com ■ ₹₹₹
Built in the early 1900s and nestled close to the city's leafy Civil Lines area, this beautiful white heritage building, with its Colonial architectural style, retains a strong old-world charm.

The Taj Mahal Hotel
MAP P4 ■ 1 Man Singh Road ■ 6656 6162 ■ www.taj.tajhotels.com ■ ₹₹₹
A lobby with Art Deco marble floors, fountains and beautiful mini-domes greets visitors to this hotel. The rooms are just as impressive, with decor that is a blend of traditional and contemporary.

The Taj Palace
MAP K4 ■ 2 Sardar Patel Marg, Diplomatic Enclave ■ 2611 0202 ■ www.tajhotels.com ■ ₹₹₹
This grand building is set within lovely lawns and has striking interiors. Relax at the nine-hole chip-and-putt golf green or work out at the state-of-the-art fitness centre.

Vivanta by Taj – Ambassador

MAP P5 ▪ Sujan Singh Park, Subramaniam Bharti Marg ▪ 6626 1000 ▪ www.vivanta.tajhotels.com/en-in/ambassador-new-delhi ▪ ₹₹₹

This centrally located hotel offers comfortable and stylish rooms, with classic interiors. The many highlights of staying here include a fitness centre that offers yoga, a popular on-site restaurant and a lovely breakfast buffet.

Boutique Hotels

Amarya Villa

MAP V1 ▪ A-2/20 Safdarjung Enclave ▪ 4175 9267 ▪ www.amaryagroup.com ▪ ₹₹

Conveniently located, this hotel is set away from the bustling crowds. It offers a range of spacious and stylish guestrooms that have been themed around the "Navratna", India's nine traditional auspicious gemstones.

B Nineteen

MAP S6 ▪ B-19 Nizamuddin (East) ▪ 98710 88629 ▪ www.bnineteen.com ▪ ₹₹

A gorgeous boutique hotel, this blends tasteful contemporary style with traditional decor and lovely wooden furniture. The service is non-intrusive, the food excellent and the location is top notch.

Colonel's Retreat

MAP W1 ▪ D-418 Defence Colony ▪ 4660 4927 ▪ www.colonelsretreat.com ▪ ₹₹

Calling itself Delhi's "best-kept secret", this charming accommodation option feels a bit like staying in a friend's home. The terrace is the perfect place to relax and read a book or enjoy a meal.

Haveli Dharampura

MAP G4 ▪ 2293 Gali Guliyan, Dharampura, near Jama Masjid Gate No. 3, Chandni Chowk ▪ 2326 1000 ▪ www.havelidharampura.com ▪ ₹₹

Set in an 1887 *haveli*, this wonderfully atmospheric hotel located in the bustling alleys of Old Delhi's Chandni Chowk, a short walk from the Jama Masjid and the Red Fort. The rooms are beautiful and the service is excellent.

Haveli Hauz Khas

MAP U2 ▪ P-5 Hauz Khas Enclave ▪ 4165 1357 ▪ www.havelihauzkhas.com ▪ ₹₹

Located in the peaceful Hauz Khas Enclave residential colony, this hotel boasts five rooms, each one decorated according to a different theme, ranging from Hampi to Ajanta. One of the highlights of the place is the pleasant rooftop lounge area for guests.

Hotel Diplomat

MAP K4 ▪ 9 Sardar Patel Marg, Diplomatic Enclave ▪ 4605 0200 ▪ www.thehoteldiplomat.com ▪ ₹₹

Set amid sprawling green lawns, this hotel offers tastefully decorated rooms with contemporary interiors. The on-site restaurant, with a bistro vibe, is multi-cuisine and offers all-day breakfast and a view of the gardens.

Jaypee Vasant Continental

MAP T2 ▪ Vasant Vihar ▪ 2614 8800 ▪ www.jaypeehotels.com/vasant-continental-new-delhi ▪ ₹₹

Strategically located, this hotel blends business and leisure and offers modern accommodation. Amenities at the hotel include a swimming pool, health spa, fitness centre and a range of dining options.

JüSTa Panchsheel Park

MAP V2 ▪ S-362 Panchsheel Park ▪ 4058 2121 ▪ www.justahotels.com/panchsheel-park-new-delhi ▪ ₹₹

The 22 airy rooms here have beautiful handcrafted Burmese teak furniture and contemporary art on the walls. It's the perfect home away from home.

La Sagrita

MAP R4 ▪ 14 Sundar Nagar ▪ 2435 8572 ▪ www.lasagrita.com ▪ ₹₹

The rooms at this small but swanky boutique hotel are spacious and cool. The breakfast is excellent, and the neighbourhood is quiet and compact, tucked away between India Gate and Humayun's Tomb.

Lutyens Bungalow

MAP N6 ▪ 39 Prithviraj Road ▪ 2461 1341 ▪ www.lutyensbungalow.co.in ▪ ₹₹

Constructed in 1937, this charming bungalow is located in plush Central Delhi, strolling distance from Lodi Gardens and Safdarjung's Tomb. There is a swimming pool to relax, and the living room is furnished with books and a fireplace for cool winter evenings.

The Manor

MAP X1 ■ 77 Friends Colony (West) ■ 96433 80275 ■ www.themanor delhi.com ■ ₹₹

Delhi's first boutique hotel, this opulent establishment was opened in 1999. It is situated in a quiet corner of the upmarket Friends Colony, with the Ashram metro station within walking distance.

The Muse Sarovar Portico

MAP W2 ■ A-1 Chirag Enclave ■ 4065 0000 ■ www.musedelhi.com ■ ₹₹

Though not nearly as atmospheric as most boutique hotels in this city, the Muse is excellent for business travellers as it is located close to the Nehru Place commercial complex. Their rooms are stylish and minimalist.

Scarlette

MAP U1 ■ B2-139 Safdarjung Enclave ■ 4102 3764/65 ■ www.scarlettenewdelhi.com ■ ₹₹

This *maison d'hôte* offers four lovely rooms with French interiors blended with modern decor. It is the personal touch of the two French owners that makes this place stand out from other hotels.

Thikana

MAP V2 ■ A-7 Gulmohar Park ■ 98115 43335 ■ www.thikanadelhi. com ■ ₹₹

Enjoy a stay at this hotel that offers rooms with ethnic decor. The common areas have comfortable chairs, ideal for sinking into with a book or a drink. The property also has a lift for the ease of guests.

Roseate House

MAP A6 ■ Asset 10, Hospitality District, Aerocity ■ 7155 8800 ■ www.roseatehotels. com/newdelhi ■ ₹₹₹

Located close to the airport, this hotel offers beautiful rooms and excellent service. Guests can relax at the outdoor and indoor spa, enjoy at the movie lounge or shop at the luxury brand stores.

Mid-Range Hotels

Bajaj Indian Homestay

MAP E5 ■ 8A/34 Karol Bagh ■ 2573 6509 ■ www. indianhomestay.com ■ ₹

The clean and spacious rooms at this homestay are named after Hindu gods as well as other mythological characters. There is also a charming terrace with views.

BB Palace

MAP E5 ■ 2638 Bank Street, Gurudwara Road, Karol Bagh ■ 4761 3500 ■ www.hotelbbpalace. com ■ ₹

A friendly place with a few pleasant rooms. See the rooms before booking – those decorated with bright colours and dark wood furniture are lovely.

Bloomrooms Hotel

MAP R7 ■ 7 Link Road, Jangpura Extension ■ 4122 5666 ■ www. bloomrooms.com ■ ₹

This is a great option located nearby popular sights such as the Lodi Gardens and Humayun's Tomb. The rooms are pleasant with minimalist decor in cheerful yellows and whites. Amici Café has a set-up here and serves all-day breakfast.

Devna

MAP R4 ■ 10 Sundar Nagar ■ 2435 5047 ■ www.devnadelhi. com ■ ₹

Surrounded by greenery and located in a lovely neighbourhood, this guesthouse offers rooms decorated with antiques and paintings. There is a state-of-the-art gymnasium next door.

Hamilton Hotel

MAP V2 ■ S-153 Panchsheel Park ■ 2601 5852 ■ ₹

Located at the edge of Panchsheel Park, the Hamilton is ideally situated for exploring South Delhi's sights. The rooms are done up in bright colours, and there is a charming porch with a fountain where guests can unwind on comfortable cane chairs.

Hotel Broadway

MAP H5 ■ 4/15-A Asaf Ali Road ■ 4366 3600 ■ www.hotelbroadway delhi.com ■ ₹

Dating back to 1956 and sandwiched between Old Delhi and Connaught Place, Hotel Broadway has a certain endearing charm. The friendly staff can arrange activities for you, ranging from performances of traditional dance to walking tours through the old city.

Hotel Florence

MAP E5 ■ 2719 Bank Street, Karol Bagh ■ 4714 4714 ■ www. florencegroup.in ■ ₹

A decent hotel offering comfortable rooms with clean en-suite bathrooms. An in-house restaurant serves Indian and some European dishes.

Ahuja Residency
MAP Q5 ▪ 193 Golf Links
▪ 2461 1027 ▪ www.
ahujaresidency.com ▪ ₹₹
Located in one of the
city's most upmarket
residential quarters,
this is a good option
for a quiet, relaxing stay.
Efficient, non-intrusive
service, beautiful room
decor that blends the
contemporary with the
traditional, a cosy dining
space and all modern
amenities make Ahuja
Residency a great place
to stay for a few days.

Hotel Palace Heights
MAP F6 ▪ D-26/28
Connaught Place ▪ 4358
2610 ▪ www.hotelpalace
heights.com ▪ ₹₹
Tastefully decorated
rooms with lovely paper
blinds and warm, woody
colours, an excellent
restaurant and a great
location are among the
few reasons to stay at
Palace Heights. The
terrace restaurant is
great for a beer and
peppery chicken tikka.

Ibis
MAP A6 ▪ Asset 9,
Hospitality District,
Delhi Aerocity ▪ 4302
0202 ▪ www.ibishotels.
com ▪ ₹₹
Set near the airport,
this chain hotel offers
comfortable rooms with
modern amenities. They
also have a sumptuous
breakfast buffet.

Budget Hotels

Blue Triangle Family Hotel (YWCA)
MAP E7 ▪ Ashoka Road
▪ 2336 5441 ▪ www.
ywcaofdelhi.org ▪ ₹
This hostel provides safe
and clean accommodation,
particularly for women.
There is a choice of
double or single rooms,
with en-suite baths and
running hot water.

Ginger Hotel
MAP G5 ▪ IRCTC – Rail
Yatra, New Delhi Railway
Station, Bhav Bhutti
Marg ▪ 6663 3333
▪ www.gingerhotels.
com ▪ ₹
Winner of the CNBC
travel award for the
Best Budget Hotel,
this place has spotlessly
clean rooms, a gym,
Wi-Fi and a restaurant.

Hotel Mint Casa
MAP X1 ▪ Mint Casa,
A-10, Friends Colony
(East) ▪ 77770 51957
▪ www.fabhotels.com ▪ ₹
The hotel has modern,
comfortable rooms and
efficient service. It is well
located for exploring the
sights of South Delhi.

Hotel New Haven
MAP W2 ▪ E-512 Greater
Kailash II ▪ 2921 8556
▪ www.nhh.in ▪ ₹
This hotel has a good
location in South Delhi
and clean rooms. Guests
can head to the nearby
Greater Kailash market
to choose from a variety
of food options.

Hotel Tara Palace
MAP H4 ▪ 419 Esplanade
Road, Chandni Chowk
▪ 2327 6465 ▪ www.tara
palacedelhi.com ▪ ₹
With friendly service
and a great location in
the heart of Old Delhi,
Hotel Tara Palace is the
perfect starting point
for exploring Chandni
Chowk. Both the Red
Fort and Jama Masjid
are within walking
distance of this hotel.

International Youth Hostel
MAP K5 ▪ 5 Nyaya Marg,
Chanakyapuri ▪ 2611
6285 ▪ www.yhaindia.
org ▪ ₹
This is a huge favourite
among young budget
travellers for its location
and facilities. Choose
from a range of dorms, or
double rooms with shared
or private bathrooms.

Madpackers
MAP V2 ▪ 3rd floor,
S-39A Panchsheel Park
▪ 98186 71874 ▪ ₹
Conveniently located
close to a metro station,
this informal hostel has
dorms, including one just
for women, making it a
good choice for female
travellers. There are
plenty of communal
spaces, including a
kitchen and a terrace.

Metropolis Tourist Home
MAP F5 ▪ 1634, Main
Bazar Road, Paharganj
▪ 2356 1782 ▪ www.
metropolistouristhome.
com ▪ ₹
Owing to its excellent
location and friendly service, the Metropolis has
fast become a popular
budget option among
backpackers. Located
in the middle of busy
Paharganj, it also has a
great terrace restaurant.

Stops
MAP H5 ▪ 4/23-B Asaf
Ali Road ▪ 4105 6226
▪ www.stopshostels.
com ▪ ₹
Join the backpacker
crowd at this cool
hostel on the southern
edge of Old Delhi near
Delhi Gate. There's a
kitchen, bar, dorms
and private rooms.

YMCA

MAP F7 ■ Jai Singh Road, Connaught Place ■ 4364 4000 ■ www.newdelhiymca.in/ndymcath ■ ₹

Since 1927, the YMCA hostel has provided excellent budget accommodation for foreign and local visitors. The rooms are basic but clean and have en-suite bathrooms. There is an Internet café and a restaurant serving traditional Indian food.

B&Bs and Guesthouses

Dawar Villa B&B

MAP G7 ■ 50 Todarmal Road, Bengali Market ■ 99113 21555 ■ www.dawarvilla.com ■ ₹

This smart, family-run B&B is situated in Bengali Market, which is famous for its lively restaurants. Dawar Villa is also close to Mandi House, one of the city's main cultural centres. The place has a warm feel to it, with gorgeous wood panelling, earthy colours and soft lighting.

Delhi B&B

MAP X1 ■ A-6 Friends Colony (East) ■ 98110 57103 ■ www.delhibedandbreakfast.com ■ ₹

Boasting bright, quirky furniture, green potted plants and lovely wall-hangings, Delhi B&B is a pleasant place to stay. Pervez and Lubna Hameed, the owners, are well travelled, speak fluent French and also offer advice on sightseeing in the city. Guests are welcome to watch the hostess prepare Indian meals.

Master Guesthouse

MAP B5 ■ R-500 New Rajendra Nagar ■ 2874 1089 ■ www.master-guesthouse.com ■ ₹

The family who run this beautifully kept little guesthouse are a mine of information on the city and their home is a delight. Breakfast is included and vegetarian meals are available.

On the House

MAP V1 ■ B-4/120 Safdarjung Enclave ■ 98110 47414 ■ www.bedandbreakfastnewdelhi.com ■ ₹

This B&B has seven rooms, named after trees, and each is decorated in vivid colours. It prides itself on its homely feel, and the home-cooked food here is delicious. It is a favourite with solo women travellers.

Sai Villa B&B

MAP W2 ■ E-578 Greater Kailash II ■ 98110 69943 ■ www.saivilla.com ■ ₹

It may not be the most stylish of guesthouses, but Sai Villa offers clean, spacious rooms, well-equipped, en-suite bathrooms, attentive staff and a prime location. The B&B also has deals with a number of nearby restaurants, so guests can ask to have meals delivered to their door.

Saket B&B

MAP V3 ■ 3rd Floor, D-21 Saket ■ 95828 72580 ■ ₹

Located within a walking distance to the metro station and a short distance from Qutb Minar, Saket B&B is a comfortable option with spacious, well-maintained rooms and en-suite bathrooms.

The popular malls Select Citywalk and DLF Place Saket are also easily accessible from here.

Tree of Life

MAP V3 ■ D-193 Saket ■ 98102 77699 ■ www.tree-of-life.in ■ ₹

There are seven spotless, spacious rooms, along with a lounge and kitchen, at this friendly little guesthouse in a quiet neighbourhood near the Qutb Minar, a short walk from Saket metro station.

Trendy B&B

MAP R7 ■ 9-B Mathura Road, Jangpura ■ 98100 19060 ■ www.trendybb.com ■ ₹

Situated close to the Nizamuddin metro station, this B&B has a cosmopolitan feel. The owner is well-travelled and has a network of friends across the globe. The rooms are spotlessly clean and spacious.

Vandana's B&B

MAP V1 ■ B-4/124 Safdarjung Enclave ■ 93129 42834 ■ www.bedandbreakfastnewdelhi.in ■ ₹

A warm, cosy family-run B&B, this boasts a charming rooftop garden, perfect for breakfast in the winter sun or a chilled drink in the summer.

11 Nizamuddin

MAP S6 ■ 11 Nizamuddin (East) ■ 98110 88966 ■ www.elevendelhi.com ■ ₹₹

Set in an elegant Colonial bungalow with a lawn, the rooms are charming, elegantly furnished and uncluttered. The area is smart, peaceful, quiet and close to several heritage monuments such as the grand Humayun's Tomb. There is a gym and a mini sports-complex nearby.

76 Friends Colony
MAP X1 ▪ 76 Friends Colony (West) ▪ 4145 4681 ▪ www.76friends colonywest.com ▪ ₹₹
This elegant B&B has cosy and well-ventilated rooms with basic amenities. The staff is friendly and helpful. Guests can relax in the lovely terrace garden.

G 49 Nizamuddin
MAP R6 ▪ G-49 Nizamuddin (West) ▪ 4737 3449 ▪ www.bed-breakfast.asia ▪ ₹₹
Tucked away in a leafy street, this is a relaxed, friendly place with elegant rooms and en-suite bathrooms. The dining area and balcony are lovely places to while away an evening.

Hotels Around Delhi

Tiger Den
MAP B3 ▪ Sariska, Alwar ▪ ₹
This state-run hotel is a great budget option for visitors to the Sariska Wildlife Sanctuary (see p73). Speak to the staff about sightseeing and safari tours in the park.

Diggi Palace
MAP B3 ▪ SMS Hospital Road, Jaipur ▪ 99290 92482 ▪ www.hotel diggipalace.com ▪ ₹₹
Built around 1727, Diggi Palace hosts a number of cultural events, including the annual Jaipur Literary Festival, which draws in writers from all over the globe. The hotel itself is

charming, with pretty fountains and rooms that hint at a glorious past.

Glasshouse on the Ganges
MAP C2 ▪ 23rd Milestone, Rishikesh–Badrinath Road, Gular–Dogi ▪ 09412 0764 20 ▪ www.glass house-on-the-ganges. neemranahotels.com ▪ ₹₹
Located in a fruit orchard, this hotel has six cottages overlooking the tumbling Ganges. Ask the staff about booking activities such as fishing, trekking and white-water rafting.

Hill Fort Kesroli
MAP B3 ▪ Kesroli, near MIS Post Office, Bahala, Alwar ▪ 98294 99901 ▪ www.the-hill fort-kes roli.neemranahotels.com ▪ ₹₹
Set in an atmospheric 14th-century fort perched on a rocky outcrop, this charming little hotel offers splendid views of the surrounding mustard fields. The rooms are cool, with high ceilings, and are elegantly decorated in traditional style.

ITC Mughal
MAP C3 ▪ Taj Ganj, Agra ▪ 056 2402 1700 ▪ www. itcwelcomgroup.in ▪ ₹₹
This resort houses the country's largest spa. After a tiring day's sightseeing, relax in a private hammam (Turkish bath).

Kadamb Kunj
MAP C3 ▪ NH 11, Fatehpur Sikri, Bharatpur ▪ 92142 04489 ▪ www. kadambkunj.in ▪ ₹₹
Located not far from the Keoladeo Ghana National Park (see p72), the Kadam Kunj is very popular with birdwatchers.

Neemrana Fort-Palace
MAP B3 ▪ 122nd Milestone Delhi–Jaipur Highway, Neemrana, Alwar ▪ 0124 466 6166 ▪ www.fort-palace.neem ranahotels.com ▪ ₹₹
Carved into a hillside, this architectural jewel is steeped in history. Guests can try the pool, which offers amazing views of the countryside, or indulge in rejuvenating Ayurvedic spa treatments.

The Oberoi Amarvilas
MAP C3 ▪ Taj East Gate Road, Agra ▪ 0562 2231 515 ▪ www.amarvilas. com ▪ ₹₹₹
Constructed in a Moorish- and Mughal-inspired style, this gorgeous five-star property, not far from the Taj Mahal, is a beautiful place to stay.

Rambagh Palace
MAP B3 ▪ Bhawani Singh Road, Jaipur ▪ 0141 2385 700 ▪ www.tajhotels.com ▪ ₹₹₹
Built in 1835, Rambagh Palace was once the residence of Maharaja of Jaipur. An elegant air surrounds the lavish grounds of this property, also known as the "Jewel of Jaipur".

Tikli Bottom
MAP B3 ▪ Gairatpur Baas, PO Tikli, Gurugram ▪ 93133 70853 ▪ www. tiklibottom.com ▪ ₹₹₹
About an hour from Delhi lies this country hotel, owned by former British diplomats who stayed on after their posting in India. A Lutyens-style bungalow built around a courtyard, the house has a swimming pool and an organic farm.

General Index

Acknowledgments

The Authors

Gavin Thomas is a London-based travel writer specializing in the Gulf, Sri Lanka and, especially India. He is the author of *The Rough Guide to Dubai*, *The Rough Guide to Sri Lanka*, co-author of *The Rough Guide to Rajasthan, Delhi and Agra* and a contributing author to *The Rough Guide to India*.

Janice Pariat is a freelance writer based in Shillong. She has lived and worked in Delhi for almost a decade and loves the city's clash of culture, pace and climate. She writes travel stories for *HT City* (Mumbai) and *Travel to Care*, a website dedicated to eco-tourism.

Additional contributor
Daniel Jacobs

Publishing Director Georgina Dee

Publisher Vivien Antwi

Design Director Phil Ormerod

Editorial Ankita Awasthi Tröger, Michelle Crane, Dipika Dasgupta, Rachel Fox, Shikha Kulkarni, Maresa Manara, Ruth Reisenberger, Sally Schafer

Cover Design Maxine Pedliham, Vinita Venugopal

Design Hansa Babra, Tessa Bindloss, Bharti Karakoti, Rahul Kumar, Ankita Sharma, Priyanka Thakur, Vinita Venugopal

Picture Research Subhadeep Biswas, Taiyaba Khatoon, Ellen Root, Rituraj Singh

Cartography Mohammad Hassan, Stuart James, Jasneet Kaur, Suresh Kumar, Casper Morris, Animesh Kumar Pathak

DTP Jason Little, George Nimmo, Azeem Siddiqui, Ajay Verma, Tanveer Zaidi

Production Jude Crozier

Factchecker Avantika Sukhia

Proofreader Clare Peel

Indexer Helen Peters

Revisions Gaurav Joshi, Kanika Praharaj, Stuti Tiwari, Vaishali Vashisht

Commissioned Photography Idris Ahmed, Dinesh Khanna

Picture Credits

Kingshuk Ghoshal: 71clb.

Indian Accent: Rohit Chawla 64ca.

iStockphoto.com: amlanmathur 51br; Jayesh 25clb; JDMaddox 31bc; JeremyRichards 21bl; Alan Lagadu 87tl; Meinzahn 18–9; Harjeet Singh Narang 17c, 60t, Soumen Nath 18cla; powerofforever 25tl; Saiko3p 24cla; SoumenNath 46tl.

National Railway Museum, India: photo Dorling Kindersley Ltd/Deepak Aggarwal 95cl.

Old World Hospitality Pvt. Ltd.: 89cr.

PENGUIN and the Penguin logo are trademarks of Penguin Books Ltd: *The Last Mughal* by William Dalrymple 57bl; *Delhi: Adventures in a Megacity* by Sam Miller 56cb.

Robert Harding Picture Library: Peter Barritt 45br.

Sulabh International Museum of Toilets: 55c.

The Park New Delhi: 65br, 82t.

The Shop: 81cla.

The Taj Mahal Hotel, New Delhi: 83crb.

Cover

Front and spine: **AWL Images:** Nigel Pavitt.

Back: **Alamy Stock Photo:** Jon Arnold Images Ltd crb, Purepix tr, TMI cla; **AWL Images:** Nigel Pavitt bc; **iStockphoto.com:** mariusz_prusaczyk tl.

Pull Out Map Cover
AWL Images: Nigel Pavitt.

All other images © Dorling Kindersley
For further information see:
www.dkimages.com

*As a guide to abbreviations in visitor information blocks: **Adm** = admission charge.*

Penguin
Random
House

Printed and bound in China

First edition 2010

Published in Great Britain
by Dorling Kindersley Limited
80 Strand, London WC2R 0RL

Published in the United States by
DK US, 1450 Broadway, Suite 801
New York, NY 10018, USA

Copyright © 2010, 2019 Dorling
Kindersley Limited

A Penguin Random House Company

19 20 21 22 10 9 8 7 6 5 4 3 2 1

Reprinted with revisions 2012, 2014, 2019

ISSN 1479-344X

ISBN 978-0-2413-6802-2

SPECIAL EDITIONS OF DK TRAVEL GUIDES

MIX
Paper from
responsible sources
FSC™ C018179
www.fsc.org

Selected Street Index